HOW TO BREAK YOUR ADDICTION TO A PERSON

HOW TO BREAK YOUR ADDICTION TO A PERSON

Howard M. Halpern, Ph.D.

McGRAW-HILL BOOK COMPANY

New York   St. Louis   San Francisco
Toronto   Hamburg   Mexico

1 2 3 4 5 6 7 8 9 DO DO 8 7 6 5 4 3 2

ISBN 0-07-025627-6

LIBRARY OF CONGRESS CATALOGING IN PUBLICATION DATA

Halpern, Howard Marvin, 1929–
How to break your addiction to a person.
1. Separation (Psychology)   2. Autonomy
(Psychology) I. Title.
BF575.G7H34   158′.2   81-20740
ISBN 0-07-025627-6   AACR2

Book design by Judy Allan

CONTENTS

INTRODUCTION

It can be very hard to end a love relationship, even when you know it is bad for you.

When I refer to a relationship that is bad for you I am *not* referring to a relationship that is going through the difficult periods of discord and disenchantment that are an inescapable part of the process of two separate and changing people struggling to maintain a loving partnership.

I *am* talking about relationships that are dead ends.

I am talking about attachments to people who are painfully unattainable (perhaps because they are committed to someone else, or don't want a committed relationship, or are incapable of one).

I am talking about mismatched relationships where the two partners are basically on such different wavelengths that there is little common ground, little important communication, little enjoyment of each other or with each other.

I am talking about relationships that are chronically lacking in what one or both partners need and want, be it love or tenderness or sexuality or stimulation or honesty or respect or emotional support.

In some instances I am talking of relationships that are wastelands of emptiness, distance, loneliness and deprivation.

And in some instances I am talking of relationships that are battlegrounds of hatred, rage and abuse.

Remaining in a bad relationship can be an ongoing personal tragedy. Often, the reason people do not find a satisfying relationship is their inability to let go of an irreparably unsatisfying one and move on.

This book is offered as a guide to all those who are stuck in bad relationships and wish they were not. I will try to unravel the puzzle of what it is that makes people stay in such relationships. And I will try to show them the way out.

While I write primarily for those who are in bad *central* relationships, as with a lover or spouse, the principles I develop can be used equally well with friends, relatives, employees, jobs, etc.

I gratefully dedicate this book to the many patients and friends who have shared the struggles of their relationships with me. It is from them that I have learned much of what I now pass along to you.

I give special thanks to Lori Jacobs for the preparation of the manuscript, to Ellen Levine, my agent and friend, for her consistent and helpful backing and to Jane H. Goldman for her caring and her incisive and invaluable suggestions.

Howard Halpern, Ph.D.

HOW TO BREAK YOUR ADDICTION TO A PERSON

1

PRISONER OF LOVE?

Maybe the Surgeon General hasn't determined it yet, but staying in a bad relationship may be dangerous to your health. It can shake your self-esteem and destroy your self-confidence as surely as smoking can damage your lungs. When people say that their relationship with their partner—a lover or spouse—is killing them, it may be true. The tensions and chemical changes caused by stress can throw any of your organ systems out of kilter, can drain your energy, and lower your resistance to all manner of unfriendly bugs. And often it can drive one to the overuse of unhealthy escapes, such as alcohol, amphetamines, barbiturates, narcotics, tranquilizers, reckless pursuits, and even overt suicidal acts.

But even if there were no threat to your health, staying too long in a relationship that is deadening, or deadly, can cloud your life with frustration, anger, emptiness, and despair. You may have tried to improve it, to breathe life back into it, but you have found that your efforts have been futile—and demoralizing. You are certainly not alone. Many basically rational and practical people find that they are unable to leave a relationship even though they can see that it is bad for them. Their best judgment and their self-respect tell them to end it, but often, to their dismay, they hang on. They speak and act as if something were holding them back, as if their relationship was a prison and they were locked in. Friends and psychotherapists may have pointed out to them that in reality their "prison door" is wide open and that all they need do is step outside. And yet as desperately unhappy as they are, they hold back. Some of them approach the threshold, then hesitate. Some may make brief sallies outside, but quickly retreat to the safety of prison in relief and despair. Something in them wants out. Something in them knows that they were not meant to live this way. Yet people, in droves, choose to remain in their prisons, making no effort to change them—except, perhaps, to hang pretty curtains over the bars and paint the walls in decorator colors. They may end up dying in a corner of their cell without having really been alive for years.

Every day I listen to the struggles of men and women who feel imprisoned in unsatisfying relationships.

Alice: I'm slowly growing crazy with Burt. He's so cut off from his feelings and so unresponsive to me that I feel I'm with a robot. In the beginning he was kind of romantic, but now there's nothing coming from him but silence and disinterest. When I complain he says that's the way he is. Even though I'm so frustrated and miserable, I can't get myself to leave him. In fact, I get very frightened when I think about it seriously. . . .

Jason: Dee is irresponsible and selfish much of the time. She'll put me down before other people and sometimes flirt with other men right in front of me. If I get annoyed, she accuses me of trying to suffocate her, but I've checked it out with my friends and they say that she really does give me a hard time—so much so that they sometimes wince for me. At this point, I can't see anything she gives me, yet whatever is binding me to her seems stronger than I am.

Maureen: I know Brad will never leave his wife. I see that I'm destroying myself and wasting years of my life by staying involved with him, but each time I've tried to end it, the hell I went through was unbearable and back I would go. . . . I feel he owns me.

Mitchell: I don't know how it happens, but everything is a battle, an awful gut-twisting fight. We get into power struggles over every little thing, from what movie to see to how much the window should be opened. I think the only thing Lara and I agree on is that we'd be better off without each other, but we can't let go.

Jo Anne: I stopped loving Dennis years ago. Most nights, I dread his coming home. But we have so much together—the house, the kids, memories, and maybe just plain habit—so that as much as I want out, the thought of his no longer being in my life and of all I'd have to go through to end it makes me hang in there for another year, and then another year, and another. I'm becoming resigned that this is all there is for me, but I feel dead. . . .

Arthur: The truth is, I don't love Betsy, at least not enough to marry her, but I can't break it off. . . . I avoid meeting new women because I expect them to reject me, and that possibility terrifies me. So I guess I hold on to Betsy because she's there. I like knowing that at least there is someone who really cares about whether I get hit by a truck and who I can share all those little things that happen during the day, like just missing my bus or getting a new shirt—things that nobody else would give a damn about.

Eileen: Why do I keep seeing Peter when he treats me

3

so badly? He's really cruel to me, and totally self-centered. I practice telling him it's over in a hundred ways. "I love you, but the relationship is not good for me." "This isn't working." "I don't want to see you any more." "I've outgrown my need for you." "Get lost, you selfish SOB." "Drop dead." And sometimes I do say these things and I do end it—for a week!

THE POWER OF SELF-DECEPTION

All of these people really believe it would be better for them to leave the relationship, but when it comes to doing so they are paralyzed. In order to remain in the relationship, knowing it is against their own best interests, they frequently try to trick themselves by distorting the situation. They rationalize, using "good" reasons to conceal other possibly unconscious reasons.

Alice (who is "slowly going crazy" with Burt's distance and disinterest): I know he really loves me beneath his coldness. He just has difficulty showing it. Why else would he not want to break up?

Jason (who finds Dee selfish and hurtful): I know she often seems cruel and insensitive, but maybe it's just that I'm being too sensitive and expecting too much.

Maureen (who knows Brad will never leave his wife): Sometimes it feels so good between us, and he seems so loving that I can't believe he'd be stupid enough to stay with her.

Mitchell (who fights with Lara about every little thing): Maybe the fact that we fight so much shows how much we love each other.

Jo Anne (who stopped loving Dennis long ago): Maybe love isn't very important. Maybe this is all there really is for anyone.

Arthur (who doesn't love Betsy enough to marry her): There aren't many women out there whom I would be attracted to and who would be attracted to me.

Eileen (who finds Peter treats her cruelly): It's not that he doesn't love me. He's just afraid of commitment.

Rationalization is not the only self-deceptive technique. People sometimes hold deeply entrenched *feelings* and *beliefs* that defy logic and, worse, can blur judgment as to what is in one's own healthy self-interest.

Alice: If I leave Burt, I know I'll be alone forever, and that's the most frightening thing I can imagine.

Jason: Dee often treats me like dirt. Every word is a complaint, a criticism, or a command. But I love her. I feel I couldn't live without her.

Maureen: Sometimes I have this fantasy that I'll marry someone else, and Brad will stay with his wife but that we will remain lovers forever. It's in our stars.

Mitchell: I know that we can't talk for two minutes without fighting, but when you feel the way I do about Lara, you can always work it out.

Jo Anne: Every time I think of leaving I feel overcome by guilt.

Arthur: Who else would want me?

Eileen: Peter says he doesn't love me any more, but it just can't be. He loved me once, and it just doesn't disappear. He has to love me.

Some of these statements may sound so familiar it is hard to see what's wrong with them. You've heard them from people you know. You've read them in romantic novels. You've heard them in films, plays, and songs. Perhaps you are using them now to barter away your happiness. If you are, you must ask: What are you protecting? What are you afraid of? What are the *real* reasons that lie behind the "good" reasons?

5

"SOMETHING TAKES HOLD OF ME"

Eileen is an attractive and talented twenty-eight-year-old editor of a woman's magazine. She had come to see me for psychotherapy because her physician had told her that her skin rashes and difficulty sleeping were emotional in origin. For the past two years she had been involved with Peter, a dynamic and successful architect, and it was during this time that her symptoms had developed. It was easy to see why. At best, Peter treated her badly. Often he was cruel. And Eileen would put up with his treatment. They would have a date, and he'd fail to show up. Then he might call about 2 A.M., make a weak excuse, and tell her to "grab a cab and come over." And she would get out of bed, dress, and take a taxi to his apartment.

In one session Eileen came in glowing because Peter, uncharacteristically, had asked her to go away with him to a resort for the weekend. But at the next session she was depressed and bitter. As they were on their way to what she had believed would be a romantic holiday, Peter informed her that he would be attending a business conference and that she would be alone most of the time. She had been furious, she yelled at him and cried, but, as so often before, he just accused her of being too demanding. When they returned from the weekend, she told him that she couldn't take it any more and that she didn't want to see him again. He shrugged and left. In less than a week, in five days of agony, sleeplessness, despair and a blotchy rash, she found herself dialing his number, willing to go back on the most humiliating terms. "It's like something takes hold of me," she cried.

What is it that takes hold of her? Why does this capable and otherwise rational woman remain so intensely involved with a man who is consistently rejecting, who repeatedly causes her pain? Why, when she tries to give up this relationship, does she experience even more acute torment?

ADDICTION TO A PERSON

Looked at closely, Eileen's attachment to Peter has all the characteristics of an *addiction*. I am not using the term "addiction" symbolically or metaphorically. Not only is it possible but it is extremely common for one person in a love relationship to become addicted to the other. Stanton Peele, in his book *Love and Addiction,* recognized the addictive nature of some love relationships. Reviewing many studies of drug addiction he noted a frequent conclusion—that the addicting element is not so much in the substance (such as alcohol or tobacco or a narcotic) but *in the person who is addicted.* In love relationships, this addictive element takes the form of a compelling need to connect with and to remain connected with a particular person. But is this need always an addiction? Why call it an addiction at all? Why not simply call it love or preference or a sense of commitment?

Often there *is* a lot of love and commitment in an addictive relationship, but to be genuinely loving and committed one must *freely choose* another person, and one of the hallmarks of an addiction is that it is a *compulsive* drive which, by definition, means that it limits this freedom. The alcoholic or drug addict feels driven toward the addictive substance even when he knows it is bad for him. And when there is a strong addictive element in a relationship, the feeling is "I must have this person, and I must remain attached to this person, even if this relationship is bad for me."

So the first indication that we are dealing with an addiction is its compulsive quality. The second is the *panic* one feels at the possible absence of the substance. Alcoholics often feel panic when they are not

7

sure where the next drink is coming from. Drug addicts experience this fear when their supply of drugs is running out. Nicotine addicts may become very uneasy about being in a place where smoking is not permitted. And people in an addictive relationship may experience overwhelming panic at the thought of breaking the relationship. I have often heard of people sitting at the telephone and beginning to dial the number of their partner in an unhappy love affair, determined to tell him or her that it is all over, but their anxiety becomes so great they have to hang up.

The third hallmark of an addiction is the *withdrawal symptoms*. As bad as the panic is in contemplating or moving toward a possible breakup, it cannot compare to the devastation when the breakup actually happens. A person who has just ended an addictive relationship may suffer greater agony than drug addicts, smokers, and alcoholics endure when they go cold turkey, and in many ways the reaction is similar. Often, for example, there is physical pain (the chest, stomach, and abdomen are particularly reactive), weeping, sleep disturbances (some people can't sleep, others may sleep too much), irritability, depression, and the feeling that there is no place to go and no way to end the discomfort except to go back to the old substance (person). The craving can become so intense it often defeats the sufferer's best intentions and drives him right back to the source of his addiction.

The fourth hallmark of an addiction is that after the mourning period, there is often a sense of liberation, triumph, and accomplishment. This differs from the slow, sad acceptance and healing that follows a non-addictive loss.

Underlying all these reactions, the essential similarity between addicts, whether their addiction is to a substance or a person, is *a sense of incompleteness, emptiness, despair, sadness, and being lost that he believes he can remedy only through his connection to something or someone outside himself*. This something or *someone* becomes the center of his existence, and he is willing to do himself a great deal of damage to keep his connection with it intact.

If we look back at Eileen's tie to Peter, we can see many of the signs of addiction. She feels *compelled* to be in contact with him, she *panics* when she thinks about ending it, and has intense and agonizing *withdrawal* symptoms, including physical disturbances from which she can only find immediate relief by reestablishing a connection with him. And despite her considerable accomplishments and her many appealing qualities, she has serious doubts about whether she is within herself a complete, adequate, and lovable person if she is without her connection to Peter.

ARE YOU ADDICTED?

There is probably an addictive element in every love relationship, and that, in itself, need not be bad. It can, in fact, add strength and delight to the relationship. After all, who is so complete, so self-contained, so "healthy" and "mature" that he doesn't need to feel good about himself through a close tie with another person? In fact, one sign of a good relationship is that it puts us in touch with the best in ourselves. What makes a particular relationship an addiction is when these little addictive "I need you" elements expand to become the controlling force in your attachment. This creates an inner coercion that deprives you of several essential freedoms: the freedom to be your best self in the relationship, the freedom to love the other person through choice and caring commitment rather than being compelled by your own dependence, and the freedom to choose whether to stay with the other person or to leave.

If you are deeply unhappy in a love relationship, and yet you remain in it, how can you determine whether your decision to stay is based on preference and commitment or if you are addicted? There are several signs of addiction that you can look for in yourself:

1. Even though your objective judgment (and perhaps the judgment of others) tells you that the relationship is bad for you and you cannot expect any improvement, you take no effective steps to break with it.

2. You give yourself reasons for staying in it that do not hold water or that are not really strong enough to balance the negatives in the relationship.

3. When you think about ending the relationship, you feel dread, even terror, and you cling to it even harder.

4. When you take steps to end it, you suffer acute withdrawal symptoms, including physical distress, that can only be relieved by reestablishing contact.

5. When the relationship is *really* over (or you fantasize that it has ended), you feel the lostness, aloneness, and emptiness of a person eternally exiled—often followed or even accompanied by a feeling of liberation.

If most of these signs are there, you can be quite certain that you are in a relationship where the addictive elements have become so large and so controlling that they destroy your capacity to direct your own life. And, in the same way an alcoholic must begin the journey to sobriety by admitting "I am an alcoholic," you must begin with the recognition that you are indeed hooked. That is the essential first step in understanding the basis of your addiction, in seeing how it works, and in becoming free enough of it so that you can decide whether you wish to work to improve the relationship, to accept it as it is, or, if you can neither improve it nor accept it, to leave it.

I

ATTACHMENT HUNGER – THE BASIS OF ADDICTION

2

THE LOVE FIX

If you suspect that you are staying in a bad relationship because you are addicted to it, then it is essential that you understand the roots of your addiction. Otherwise, you are likely to compound the problem by being self-critical, condemning your addiction as a weakness or a humiliating fault. Or you may decide that, since it is an addiction, you might as well go on with it because, after all, it's bigger than you are. But if you know how your addiction evolved, you will be able to see it as a logical and understandable development in your history, to take a compassionate attitude toward it, and learn what you can do to overcome it.

LEVELS OF LINKAGE

There are three psychological "levels of linkage" that can influence your decision to stay in a relationship that you know you should leave. At the top level are the Practical Considerations for not leaving, and because they are the most obvious of the levels, they are the most easily understandable and observable. For example, there are seemingly overwhelming issues in ending a destructive marriage where there are young children or when there is financial dependence or where there is such an intricate and long-standing entanglement that a breakup would cause great disruption in the lives of all involved.

The second layer down are the Beliefs you hold about relationships in general, about your specific troubled relationship, and about yourself. In part, these Beliefs are composed of learned societal injunctions and clichés such as: "Love conquers all," "Love is forever," "Marriage is a sacrament and unbreakable," "The most important thing is security," "The Devil you know is better than the Devil you don't know," "Ending a relationship is a failure," "Being alone is a humiliation," "You must never hurt or disappoint anyone," "Not being a couple is being half a scissors," etc. And then there are the beliefs about one's self, such as: "I'm not attractive enough," "I'm not smart enough," "I'm not interesting enough," "I'm not successful enough"—therefore, "No one else would want me so I'd better stay where I am." And besides, "I'm not competent enough to manage on my own."

Finally, there is the deepest level of feelings and motives that can keep you stuck. This level originates early, often operates beneath your awareness and can, from its hidden recesses, control your life. This level exists in everyone in varying degrees, and its emotional power can be much greater than the levels of Practical Considerations and Beliefs. This primal layer is the level of Attachment Hunger. And it is this level that we will be exploring because *Attachment Hunger is the basis of being addicted to another person.* It is so powerful that it can completely override Practical Considerations ("This relationship is bad for my health") and Beliefs ("A person should leave a loveless and limiting relationship") that oppose it.

The roots of your attachment needs are easy to understand. Everyone started as a helpless infant. On your own you could not do even the most rudimentary things for your own comfort or survival. You had recently come from a place where your comfort and safety were so complete that you would never know such encompassing bliss and security again. Thrust out into the world, you certainly could not cope by yourself either with the demands from without or the chaotic feelings from within. Your impulse must have been to go right back to the safety and warmth, but obviously you could not. You did, however, have a mother, and she, probably, responded to your needs in a way that did three things: (1) It kept you alive and well, (2) It gave you the illusion of being in a safe, satisfying, womblike situation, and (3) It gave you, through the symbiotic merger with this powerful person, the illusion that you were enormously powerful. This is very heady stuff and not easily surrendered, either in the face of your own innate desire to become a separate person or your mother's attempt to wean you. It is understandable that you would hold onto her tightly.

In the last several decades, studies have been reported on the importance of the infant's need to attach himself to the mothering one with his hands, his arms, and his eyes. It is a deep, biological need, and how the mothering person responded to that need at a very early age will have a great impact on an adult's ability both to form a good primary relationship as well as his ability to live without one when that may be necessary or wise. Even the most devoted of mothers cannot be perfectly tuned in to the child, cannot be with him at every moment, cannot be always and immediately responsive to his needs. The most devoted mother still has other things to take care of and has her own needs, worries, and preoccupations. She may be depressed, tense, or physically ill. She may hold certain attachment-frustrating Beliefs (*e.g.*, that it is bad to pick up a baby when he cries or to feed him off schedule). She may need to be away at times. These factors can interrupt the attachment bond and may leave a lasting trace of Attachment Hunger in her child.

The more an infant's attachment needs are gratified in this early stage the better, particularly in the first year or two of life. But it is not only faulty gratification of these needs that can lead to residual Attachment Hunger but deficiencies on the part of either parent in *launching* the child, in helping him to move away from his safe and warm symbiosis with mother. Good launching gives a child backing and builds his confidence. It teaches him that he can stand up on his own and take some risks. It shows him that the world is not malevolent and filled mainly with dangers, and that he has the ability both to cope with it alone and to find new relationships with people other than his parents. Often, mothers who are superbly responsive in the *attachment* phase, perhaps because of their own needs to hold on to the closeness with their child, do a very poor job in this launching phase, holding on to the child, undermining his efforts at autonomy, fearful of his risk taking, resentful of his being less dependent. The role of the father is particularly crucial here.

Mother's willingness to help the child detach, first by letting him be sufficiently attached and filled with the assurance of her caring presence, then by permitting him to take steps away from her, to come back, and to step out again, is crucial to the development of his autonomy. But both mother and child often need help, the mother because she may have deep needs of her own to hold on to the child, the child because separation is always beset with anxiety. And here it is the father who must take the child by the hand and stroll with him into the larger world, showing him its joys and bedazzlement, teaching him to deal with its dangers, imparting to him the courage and confidence to be out there. At his best, the father is also available to the little child within the mother who may be upset and threatened during this time of separation. *The essential job of the father, then, is to help the mother and child separate from each other*. This is a role of quiet strength, of ordinary heroism.*

Not all fathers do this essential job well. Some fathers do not recognize that this is their job and leave all matters related to child-rearing to Mother. Some fathers may be too self-centered or too withdrawn to help the mother and child to gain some necessary distance from each other. And some fathers can be so overbearing or even cruel that they can drive their child back into the more comforting arms of Mother. A child can be made to be timid and fearful if his mother does not encourage him to take steps away from her and his father offers no alternative backing and direction.

The extent to which you, as an adult, will have strong vestiges of Attachment Hunger affecting your current relationships will depend to a great extent on what happened during these early attachment and launching phases of your development. To the degree that your parents gave you gratification in the attachment phase and then, after about the first year and a half, supported your independence, you will have less of a hangover of Attachment Hunger in your adult life. To the degree they failed to be helpful either in the attachment phase or the launching phase, you may have an intense residue of needs from the At-

* Howard Halpern, *Cutting Loose: An Adult Guide to Coming to Terms with Your Parents* (N.Y.: Simon & Schuster, 1977), p. 58. Bantam ed., 1978, p. 45.

tachment Hunger level that can compel you to seek and cling to relationships in an addictive way.

In speaking of the importance of our being weaned away from the attachment to Mother, the eminent English psychoanalyst, Winnicott, said that "it is the mother's job to disillusion the child."* He was referring to the necessity of her ending the child's illusion that they are *fused* in an omnipotent mother-child entity. The process of "disillusioning" the child is very tricky, and it is unlikely that it is ever accomplished so completely that a child will lose all illusions of reattaining that same feeling of omnipotence and total security. The desire lives on in all of us, and, for the most part, we learn to be satisfied with brief tastes of it, such as the ecstasy we may attain in sex, the high of two martinis or a joint of marijuana, the rapture of "falling in love," the delight we may derive from a work of art or music or from an awesome panorama, the exhilaration of dancing or running, and the pleasure of creating something—a poem, a painting, a melody—that never existed before. But the illusions created in order to satisfy Attachment Hunger also live on—to a much greater degree in some people than in others—in the form of the wish, the fantasy and the attempt to recapture this strength, security and bliss through fusing with another person. People express this desire in statements like:

I only feel fully alive when I'm in a close love relationship.

I feel incomplete without her. She makes me whole.

Without him I feel frightened and insecure. When he holds me I feel safe.

If I were to lose her, life would not be worth living. She is my happiness.

* D. W. Winnicott, "Transitional Objects and Transitional Phenomena," *International Journal of Psychoanalysis*, Vol. 24, 1953.

Fascinating experimental evidence of the presence and even the positive effects of gratifying this underlying attachment wish has been reported in a series of intriguing studies by Lloyd Silverman and his colleagues. The methodology in these studies is simple. The basic instrument used is a tachistoscope, an apparatus someone can look into to see a screen on which there may be projected a printed message or picture. But the message may be flashed so briefly that it is below the person's ability to see it consciously. Any response to the message would be a *subliminal perception*. In one particular study, Silverman placed an ad in a newspaper that read:

Bugged by bugs? Free treatment for cockroach or other insect phobias.

Twenty women responded to the ad. Using a technique similar to the desensitization methods of behavior therapists,

the participants were asked to visualize scenes in which they were coming into contact with whatever insects they were phobic of, these scenes ranging from the least to the most frightening. After each image was formed, the participant rated herself on a 100-point scale for the degree of discomfort experienced. When the rating was 20 or higher, instead of going on to the next step in the hierarchy, she was asked to look into the tachistoscope (and was given a subliminal message). Half of the women received *Mommy and I are one*, while the other half received a control stimulus *People are walking*. Then the women were asked to imagine the scene with the bugs and again rate the degree of discomfort. If this rating was under 20, the experimenter then went on to the next most frightening image, but if not, the same scene was repeated until the discomfort level dropped to 20.

After four desensitization sessions of this sort, the participants were reassessed for the extent of the bug phobia. On two of three measures of change (the women's ability to make contact with the insects and an observer's ratings of anxiety during these attempts at contact), there was significantly more improvement in the experimental than in the control group.*

Neither group consciously knew which message they were getting, or that they were getting any message at all.

We have evidence in this study and others that the symbiotic wish, the wish that underlies our Attachment Hunger, can be healing and calming. Obviously, this wish is a deep and powerful one. But while everyone seems to have such longings, not everyone becomes addicted to other people. *Feelings from the Attachment Hunger level will make a person an addict only if these feelings are so strong that they can override his ability to act in his own best interest.*

If your attachment needs are so great that they appear to overrule your judgment and control your actions, then it could indicate that something did go wrong in that complex process of becoming separate from that primal fusion with your mother. Maybe your mother's own Attachment Hunger need to fuse with you kept the fantasy of oneness alive till long after you should have been able to accept the reality of your separateness. Maybe she didn't effectively support your struggle to be strong and autonomous because she felt threatened by your independence from her. Or maybe she never let you experience a deep enough or lasting enough oneness with her during that early period of your life when you needed that fusion so that now you are still hungry for that insufficiently gratified symbiosis. (As Winnicott indicated, even though it is the mother's job to disillusion the child, she can never hope to succeed unless first

* L. H. Silverman, F. M. Lachmann, and R. H. Milich, *The Search for Oneness* (N.Y.: International Universities Press, 1982).

she has given him enough opportunity to have the illusion of oneness.)

Whether your dependent attachment is to a male or a female, it is likely to be based on this early and unresolved need to attain oneness with the mother of your early years. Later experiences of insufficient or disturbed loving by *either* of your parents or by others important in your life or their failure to support the development of your independence may also cause you to cling to someone now in the hope of gaining what you may feel is lacking in yourself—the ability to survive, to be safe, and to be happy. Your present clinging, then, is based on an old illusion. That illusion, as it appears in your current life, is: *The mother or father to whom you looked to make you feel good, secure, and strong exists in the person with whom you are now involved; therefore, if you can get that person to love you, everything will be okay*. Your addictive compulsion to recapture that early state of being through a connection with that special person, a person who could not possibly fulfill a need rooted in your infancy, means that you are addicted.

EILEEN'S ADDICTION

Let's look at Eileen, the young editor who is addicted to her abusive lover, from the perspective of the three psychological levels of linkage. It is clear that there is little on the level of Practical Considerations to hold her to Peter. There are no extenuating circumstances, such as economic dependence or young children. She's bright, appealing, sociable, has a good job, is well able to take care of herself, and is capable of attracting new relationships. There are no significant practical reasons for her to remain in a destructive relationship.

Looking at the second layer, the level of Beliefs, we see that Eileen clings to her unsupported Belief that Peter really loves her but simply has trouble showing it. In talking to Eileen, I discovered a romantic Belief that love will conquer all obstacles. And as far as Beliefs about herself, despite all her assets, Eileen holds strong doubts about her capacity to interest attractive men other than Peter. Some of these Beliefs are quite powerful, but if only the Practical Considerations and Beliefs levels of linkage were operating, Eileen could easily send Peter packing with no regret and much relief. But what has gotten hold of her, has taken over her perspective and her judgment, is her leftover Attachment Hunger, and it drives her to maintain the connection with Peter at all costs. It is the strength of this Attachment Hunger relative to Eileen's ability to act effectively in her own behalf either to improve the relationship or to end it that makes her tie to Peter an addiction.

ATTACHMENT OR LIMERENCE?

Eileen's relationship with Peter also had many of the qualities of what is often called "romantic love." This was particularly true at the beginning of the relationship when being with Peter and yearning for him were experiences of ecstatic joy and ecstatic pain.

Dorothy Tennov coined a new word, *limerence*,* to stand for the blissful state of walking on air, of obsessive and intrusive thoughts about the loved one, of acute longing for reciprocation, of an aching in the chest when there is uncertainty, and of seeing the loved one as utterly wonderful. Most addictive relationships start with limerence. There is an overwhelming initial attraction and excitement. There is often a feeling of having found the key to happiness. In the same sense that drug addicts speak of the

* Dorothy Tennov, *Love and Limerence* (Briarcliff, N.Y.: Stein & Day, 1979).

"rush" they get when the drug hits their bloodstream, limerence can be viewed as the "rush" of Attachment Hunger. It is the intensified and idealized essence of the illusion of oneness. This is no doubt why M. Scott Peck, in his book *The Road Less Traveled*, talks of "falling in love" (limerence) as having nothing to do with real love. He sees it as a going backward rather than a going forward.

> In some respects (but certainly not in all) the act of falling in love is an act of regression. The experience of merging with the loved one has its echoes from the time when we were merged with our mothers in infancy. Along with the merging we also reexperience the sense of omnipotence we had to give up in our journey out of childhood. All things seem possible. United with our beloved we feel we can conquer all obstacles. We believe that the strength of our love will cause the forces of opposition to bow down in submission and melt away into the darkness. All problems will be overcome. The future will be all light. The unreality of those feelings when we have fallen in love is essentially the same as the unreality of the two-year-old who feels itself to be king of the family and the world with power unlimited.*

To the extent that "falling in love" is based on the illusion of oneness it can interfere with a person's clear perceptions and honest interactions with others. But it is important to note that when it is present yet *not controlling* in a relationship, it can add a poignancy and a greater depth of feeling. The main danger is that it can also add so much power to Attachment Hunger that it can make a destructive and incompatible relationship almost unbreakable—at least until the limerence passes, which it usually will do when

---

* M. Scott Peck, *The Road Less Traveled* (N.Y.: Touchstone, 1978), p. 88.

one faces the reality of who the other person actually is.

As important as limerence can be in addiction, it is essential to note that being romantically in love or in limerence is not the same as being ruled by Attachment Hunger. Some very addictive relationships have never been limerent. And even when the feeling of limerence has long faded, a connection, a bond built of attachment needs, can still remain powerful. It is even possible for the object of your Attachment Hunger to be someone you despise, or someone who frightens, bores, or depresses you. (In fact, Eileen's limerent feeling had begun to atrophy long before she could stop clinging to Peter.)

Obviously, then, Attachment Hunger is very strong stuff. It can even outlast and overshadow the magnetic force of limerence. It can cloud your judgment, destroy your resolve and willpower, and coerce you to remain in a relationship that you know is bad for you. Attachment Hunger is the fuel of your addiction. To free yourself of its power, you must learn all you can about it and how it operates in your life.

3

THE RETURN
OF A MEMORY

In order to understand your Attachment Hunger it is essential that you realize that it is not a new experience. It is not occurring for the first time in the current relationship. It is the return of a memory. It is an emotional reminiscence of a much earlier time. Although the actual details of the memory may be largely forgotten, the *feelings* are as alive and as intense now, when they are triggered into your awareness by the loss or anticipated loss of an important connection, as when you originally felt them. And you originally felt them in the first few months and years of your life. What this means is that when you are ruled by Attachment Hunger, your state of mind is, in many ways, a re-experiencing of the state you were in as an infant or toddler. The qualities of this experience are those of a needy, vulnerable being with limited perspective, undeveloped judgment, little capacity for rational thought, and no willpower. And you need not have had a particularly traumatic or deprived childhood to have known these feelings of primitive dependency. They are part of everyone's legacy. They are deposits in everyone's memory bank. So when these Attachment Hunger states take over, your thinking and judgment are distorted and ruled by the intense emotions of a time when you were helpless.

Infant Time

Strange things happen to a person's sense of time when Attachment Hunger takes over. Since Attachment Hunger is an early childhood memory, when it is dominant it places you, in effect, on Infant Time, and Infant Time is a very different dimension from adult time. Consider:

> The infant sucks on Mother's breast and looks unwaveringly into her eyes. This blissful moment is all there is. What does he know of tomorrow? Of five minutes from now? He has "forgotten" that he was crying just a minute before. This moment, this state of being, is all-time.

Compare this with the words of a thirty-year-old woman who is very unhappy in her relationship with Jack:

> It's not often that things are good between Jack and me, but when they are and let's say we spend a weekend together, it's like a two-week vacation. Even an afternoon of lovemaking becomes timeless. I don't even think of all that's wrong between us. The good feeling is all there is.

Or consider this painful infant experience:

> He wants to be fed. He cries out. The response is not immediate. In adult time maybe it's three minutes be-

fore Mom gets the bottle warmed up. But what is that in Infant Time? A century? An eon? A boundless amount of frustration spread over an incomprehensible dimension?

Now listen to this advertising executive and note the similarity to the infant's experience:

I called and no one answered. I know it was silly, that she often doesn't get home till later, but I guess because of the argument we had I felt this twinge of anxiety. I told myself I'd call her again in half an hour, but after three minutes, three very long minutes, I dialed again. I let the phone ring twenty times. By now I was really uptight. I felt the adrenaline surge. I called every two minutes for the next hour, and each time I felt like an eternity had gone by. I looked at that stupid clock like it was mocking me, like it was stubbornly slowing down. . . .

Every infant has had an experience similar to the one below:

The baby sitter arrives. Mom and Dad get ready to go out. They tell him, though they know he cannot yet understand, that they will be back soon, in just a few hours. They leave. He screams, wails, holds his breath. They are gone. How can he know they will be back? They are gone forever. Every ticking second without them is forever.

And here are two adult counterparts:

There was an unbearable urge to call Vicki before she left for the weekend and blurt out that I didn't mean it when I said I wanted to end it, and to tell her I would go away with her as we planned. But another part of me knew that it didn't have much to do with Vicki as Vicki. It had more to do with seeing that unplanned and lonely weekend that lay ahead of me. And the forecast was for beautiful weather, which made the weekend seem longer . . . not like forty-eight hours but more like forty-eight days or forty-eight years in solitary. How do you stand up to a sentence like that?

If I end it with Wayne, I know I'll be alone forever. That's all I can see—bleakness and aloneness stretching into infinity.

These distortions in time can make you more aware of the early childhood origins of Attachment Hunger than almost any other experience. But the paradox is that once Attachment Hunger has taken hold, you do not know that you are distorting! You need to get at least one foot on solid ground outside the Attachment Hunger state to see time in more mature perspective, and to recognize how you are misshaping it. So it's when you are largely *out* of the clutches of Attachment Hunger that you must prepare for it by anticipating the time distortion and finding ways to counterpose it with adult time. The woman who said, "If I end it with Wayne, I know I'll be alone forever . . . " began to see that she only felt that way when she was in the throes of Attachment Hunger and that at other times, when her perspective was not affected by panic and was more realistic, she didn't feel quite that way. So she began to write a series of what she called "Memos to Myself." One went like this:

TO: Little Me
FROM: Big Me

If you end it with Wayne, you will feel you will be alone for all time. You will feel terrified of the eternal pain of eternal loneliness. But that's just your infant view of time. As an adult I can assure you that there is a tomorrow, and I promise you that you will feel better again.

IMPORTANT: I order you to take out this memo and read it again and again at the first sign of panic.

And another memo said:

The agony will feel like it will go on forever. It will really feel that way, and you will be tempted to get relief by calling him and starting things again. Don't! That will put you back to square one. Call a friend, take a bath, drink some wine, rearrange your closets, but don't call him. The feeling will pass.

And another:

If you can get yourself through that first seemingly endless night of despair, *and you can,* then you can get through the next night. And the pain will get less and less. The pain is not infinite. It is time limited. There is a tomorrow. Hold on, and you will have a chance for a new beginning.

Writing these memos helped. Reading them when she was overcome by pain and Infant Time helped. Not always. Sometimes she did call him, and learned again that it was a mistake. But she'd write a memo about her mistake. Gradually, she was able to stay in adult time, and from that vantage point she wondered how she could have so lost her perspective before.

Friends who know that you are trying to end a powerful addictive tie can help you to avoid taking action while in the grip of Infant Time. The man who had the "unbearable urge to call Vicki before she left for the weekend," who looked forward with horror to the forthcoming Vicki-less weekend as "forty-eight years in solitary" was about to give in to his panic and picked up the telephone to call her. But he stopped himself from calling Vicki's number and instead called a friend who knew of his struggle to break off with Vicki. "I can't stand it," he told his friend. "I'll never get through the weekend." His friend, who had experienced similar feelings at times himself, said, "Of course you can get through the weekend—it's only two days, not two centuries. Listen, tonight I'm going to a party to celebrate the opening of my brother's new store. It should be lively. How about coming along? We can talk afterward." This contact with his friend, this reassurance about the weekend not being infinite, and this invitation to the party and to talk afterward enabled him to avoid calling Vicki and to get through the weekend with much less suffering than he had anticipated.

It not only helped to restore his time perspective, but seeing that his friend was there for him also satisfied some of the neediness that rose up out of the Attachment Hunger level. This discovery made it clear that there were other people he could turn to, that he had the ability to take the initiative to reach out to them, and that there can be light and life outside of his relationship with this one person, Vicki.

I know of four women who are friends who had talked among themselves of their tendency to hold on too long to bad relationships. They made a pact to help each other with this problem. They agreed that it was all right to call each other at any time the "Attachment Hunger" was getting out of hand. One of the greatest benefits they gained was in helping each other get through an episode of panic or pain by rescuing each other from the tyranny of Infant Time. Sometimes simply hearing "You can make it through the night and you'll feel much better tomorrow—but I'm here if you need me" would not only allay the sufferer's upset but would prevent her from taking actions she would later regret. (See chapter 16.)

If this approach sounds similar to groups like Alcoholics Anonymous, it is. Alcoholics are dealing with an addiction and so are you. And AA has long been aware of the need of its members to help each other not to be overwhelmed by Infant Time, although they never refer to it as such. It is no accident that the guidebook of Al-Anon, composed of members of the families of alcoholics, is called *One Day at a Time.** If you tend to fall into a distorted time state when you end or anticipate ending a bad relationship, it is essential that you recognize that Infant Time has taken over. The more you can keep from acting on the infant time view of forever-aloneness and eternal pain, the more the panic will fade. And when that happens, adult time will again dominate, speed up, and even accelerate. The endless summers of childhood are, unfortunately, replaced by the bewilderment of "where did the summers go?" It has been said that life is like a train that starts like a local and ends as an express. So the important issue in regard to time is not that you will be alone forever or hurt forever, but that time is too precious to be squandered in the wrong relationship.

Bodily Memories

People often "recall" Attachment Hunger level feelings physically because frequently these feelings originated at a time before words, before the infant had a vocabulary to define and express these feelings. The particular body reactions will differ depending on whether the Attachment Hunger is being gratified or not. Here is a description of what it felt like to one person whose attachment needs *were* being met in a love relationship:

> When it's good between us I'm light as air. I feel sunny inside, happy. . . . I know my face is beaming like on its own accord, and I'm so relaxed, even languorous. Sometimes I stretch like a cat. . . .

One Day at a Time in Al-Anon is prepared by Al-Anon Family Group Headquarters, Inc., 1973, P.O. Box 182, Madison Square Station, New York, N.Y. 10010. It can be a valuable aid in dealing with any addictions, including to people.

(We can recognize these as the symptoms of being romantically in love, or in limerence, a frequent accompaniment of Attachment Hunger.)

But when the relationship is going badly and the attachment needs are frustrated or threatened, people describe their experiences like this:

> It is a yearning in my whole body. My mind tells me that she is clearly bad for me, but then my mind gets drowned out by this ache, mostly my stomach and chest but all over, really. It's as if my skin is longing for her skin.

> I had a dream that she left me, and I woke with my heart pounding and I was gasping for breath. My chest hurt, and I thought I might be having a coronary. I guess that's what they mean by a broken heart.

> When I first told him that it was just no good and that we had to end it, I felt relieved, but then this awful sadness came over me. There was no way to stop it. The tears just kept coming and coming, but they didn't really help. My guts are in knots, and I can't eat. I've lost five pounds in just two days. Every fiber in me wants to call him, and I have to keep reading my diary to remind myself how bad it really was with us. . . .

Attachment Hunger is composed of powerful primitive feelings that are lodged deeply in your musculature and the reactions of your body's chemistry. How can you keep yourself from being dominated by these intense physiological responses? For one thing, you can stop fooling yourself with those clichéd Beliefs that because you feel the emotional connection to the other person so intensely and so bodily (I feel it in my heart, I know it in my guts), these reactions must be telling you a great truth, must be saying what you *really* feel and want. Nothing of the kind. Your strong bodily reaction is no more *really* you than is your rationally thought-out judgment that you should break the relationship (or than those other bodily feelings of depression or tension that you experience as you remain in the relationship). The bodily reactions of Attachment Hunger simply come from a level other than your judgment, a level so early in your history that it is hardly a guide to what you, as an adult, should do. So it is essential that you *stop romanticizing* your attachment feelings if they lead you to decisions that run counter to your best interests. And you will have to keep yourself from making decisions about the relationship when in the throes of those primitive feelings. You will have to put yourself on hold until your body calms down, your head is clear, and you can regain your perspective. This is often incredibly difficult, because the bodily feelings often have a compelling intensity that can make you lose sight of the total picture and of your objectives.

Eileen spoke of Peter this way: "*Every fiber in me* wants to call him, and I have to keep reminding myself how bad it really was with us." Her strong body-emotional reaction to Peter was so powerful that when it took over it would erase her memory of all the reasons she had decided to end the relationship! She literally couldn't remember what was so bad about it (and this is a common occurrence). Or, if she did remember, she would distort her feelings about it to "It wasn't really so bad." I urged her to keep a diary of the many unhappy and destructive incidents that happened and her feelings about them as soon after they occurred as possible, so that she could look back and reclaim these memories and use them to re-experience why she had decided to end it in the first place. She did this, and at times when she longed to contact Peter and could see no reason not to, she would open her diary and slowly, often with some resistance, bring herself back to the unpleasant realities of that relationship. It reinforced her resolve very effectively. (See chapter 15 for the various writing techniques that can be used in addiction breaking.) The more she realized that her powerful physical reactions were old memories and not current truths, the more she could prevent herself from taking action on them.

4

I CAN'T LIVE WITHOUT YOU

Attachment Hunger often carries with it the feeling that holding onto or ending a particular relationship is a matter of life and death. When you think about it, that's not too surprising. You once needed someone to take care of you or you would have died, and that fact is inscribed in your neurons. Now you are biologically self-sufficient. You can take care of your own needs for food and drink and shelter and cleanliness. But the loss or anticipated loss of someone you currently feel attached to may spark old fears that your life itself is threatened. One woman expressed it this way:

When Martin left I thought I'd die. And I'm not speaking theatrically. First, I thought the pain itself would kill me, but the pain turned to deadness. I just lay in bed, didn't eat anything for days, and felt my strength ebb. I wasn't afraid to die, and I didn't particularly want to die. It just felt like the dying was happening, like I was wasting into death.

The words this woman used are similar to those used by doctors who studied the effects of "hospitalism" on very young children. The children were separated from their parents and housed in impersonal institutions where their physical needs were met but there was no holding, rocking, or cuddling, no ongoing loving contact. After screaming an initial angry protest, these infants lapsed into states of despair and detachment that became, in time, a physical wasting away of their bodies toward a frequent end point of death.

We have learned that there is a need that is almost as basic to the infant's survival as his physical requirements—the need for a caring closeness, skin against skin, and eye to eye. Depending on how well this vital need was met for you as a child, you will experience varying degrees of confidence in your ability to survive if you were to lose your connection to an importantly close person. But you need not have had as severe and traumatic an absence of nurturing intimacy as the institutionalized infants mentioned above for you to have some vestigial feelings that your life is on the line in a relationship. Even with a much more "normal" background, you may feel it to be a grim truth when you say, "I can't live without him [or her]."

The woman who said, "When Martin left I thought I'd die," actually took to bed for several months. She was too depressed to go to work or to take care of the household tasks. She had no energy or hope, and she truly experienced herself as dying. The immobilizing nature of her depression led her to begin psychotherapy with me, and in exploring her earliest relationships I learned that during the first few years of her life, her mother was very ill with an intestinal disease and was intermittently hospitalized. It was not very difficult to see the connection between her experiences of repeated abandonment at a time when her survival felt inextricably bound up in her attachment to her mother and her later collapse when Martin left her. The more she could feel this connection, the more clearly she was able to see that it was the reliving of that childhood experience of loss and terror that had now paralyzed her and that in fact she, as an adult woman, was capable of going on about her life without Martin. It was a difficult struggle for her, but she was bolstered by her growing insight. She was learning that in reality she could survive and rebuild.

Most people who feel that they may not be able to survive the loss of a love do not have as shaky a beginning as this woman and do not take to bed for months. But even without this kind of obviously insecure early history, more ordinary experiences during that period of a parent being occasionally absent, either physically or emotionally, could leave you vulnerable to the "I can't live without him/her" feeling. And *that fear can be just as powerful if you are the one who is doing the leaving as if you are the one who is left.*

So you, too, will have to differentiate the reality of your present situation from the dependency feelings that come from the Attachment Hunger level. You must begin by recognizing that your current feelings are a message about something in your early life that may have intensified your understandable childhood doubts about your ability to survive if a basic connection was broken. It is extremely helpful to focus on that period of your life. What do you know about it? Were there circumstances that might have interfered with a stable flow of survival reassurance from those closest to you? Was your mother away a lot? Was she ill? Was she particularly preoccupied by some other upsetting factors in her life? Did you "lose" her for a while through the birth of a sibling? Were both parents often unavailable? And what about you? Were you seriously ill during those early years? Were you hospitalized?

The circumstances don't have to be so specific for you to feel the need to hold onto the universal human "memory" of needing a particular other person to survive. It can be useful for you to find out and piece together all you can from that period. Ask questions. Look at photos. Try to focus your own fuzzy memories. Usually, it is the recall of an atmosphere or a mood that is most important, as with one person who said, "I can't remember anything specific, but there is a feeling that my mother was often very distraught and distracted and that I was afraid she would drop me on my head. But at other times, when she was fully there, I felt safe."

Sometimes there is a more specific memory. One man discovered that the terror he felt when he thought about ending a very destructive relationship felt exactly like the terror he could recall experiencing when he awoke one night in his crib, very thirsty, and cried out for his parents. Usually, they came quickly, but this night they didn't because they had gone out for what was probably only a brief while to their next door neighbor. He could remember the feeling that they were gone forever and he would die. He recalls that after screaming for what seemed an eternity he curled up in a corner of the crib whimpering. And he knew these were the same awful feelings he anticipated if he ended his current unhappy attachment. (This single incident did not "cause" his intense current reactions in themselves. Further exploration indicated that this "crib incident" symbolized for him an atmosphere of frequent parental emotional unavailability.)

At my suggestion, he wrote some memos to himself from the grown-up part of him that had some perspective on all this. One of them read: "Don't panic, kiddo. You're not a baby any more. You couldn't even fit in that crib. And if you were in it, and were thirsty, you could simply hop out and get yourself a glass of water or fix yourself a Bloody Mary. And you don't need Cynthia to make it for you, either. You can live without her." He was beginning to really *know* that maintaining his tie to Cynthia was not necessary for his survival.

A survey of your own early history may help you to find the areas where you may have felt survival vulnerability. Even if you can't reconstruct very much, it will help you to focus on the essential fact that the ending of your current relationship is, in truth, no threat to your life but only feels that way because it arouses emotions from a more fragile time. If you survived then, you can certainly survive now.

Existence vs. Nonexistence

There is much more to surviving as a human being than simply staying alive physically. Your attachment to the mothering person in your life was critical to your survival as a *psychological* entity, too. When you were very young, there was a period when you had not yet come to differentiate yourself as an individual apart from your mother. When your mother responded to you as a separate being, and was attuned to the language of your cry, and reflected back your smile, and talked to you and played with you and interacted with you, then you learned that you were an entity in yourself who could bring about reactions in another person. She didn't have to reflect you accurately or gratify you all the time, but if she was responsive to you much of the time, then even on those occasions when she was not responsive, she helped you to see yourself as separate from her. And Mother was not the only factor in this process. The responsiveness of the other people around you was important. Your father, by also being empathic and involved with you, was teaching you that you did not need this one person, your mother, as the sole source of your sense of existence. The alternative he offered was helpful even when Mother was empathically attuned, and was crucial if she was not. To the extent that either or both were lacking in this empathic capacity, perhaps because they simply had little of it, or were depressed or worried or self-involved, then they might not have been very good at reflecting you back to yourself in a way that would make you feel, "I am substantial enough to have an impact on another human being. I really exist."

If you have some underlying uncertainty that you exist, you may seek a sense of your existence through attaching yourself to other people to whom you give the job of rectifying your parents' failure to validate you. And should these other people also fail, you may well re-experience doubts about your existence. This is particularly true in a love relationship but can even occur in minor ways in more casual interactions. Anne was a young woman who consulted me in discouragement that her relationships with men never seemed to last. Often she ended the relationships by angrily berating and dismissing her partners for not being sufficiently responsive to her. (At other times the men ended it, accusing her of being too demanding.) But this theme came up in other interactions as well. Once she was upset because two of her co-workers were chatting when she came in and "didn't even look up to say hello. I felt, what's the matter? Don't I exist?" And at another time she came into a session saying, "What's wrong with Mickey, the elevator operator? He not only didn't greet me, but he seemed to look right through me." When we reconstructed her history it was clear that her mother suffered a post-partum depression after Anne was born and was more often depressed than not for the first few years of Anne's life. It is not difficult to imagine the countless times as an infant and child that Anne experienced her depressed mother as looking right through her and being unresponsive to her existence.

Ron, a successful writer of television dramas, often spoke of a sense of being "shattered" or "broken" when he felt that others failed to give him the support and affirmation he wanted. He desperately wanted contacts that would shore up his shaky sense of self and was often in despair when his wife was not attentive enough to his needs or responsive to his largely unspoken expectations. In the course of a therapy session, he had mentioned how difficult it was sometimes to come to grips with his feelings in the short space of a weekly session. Toward the end of the hour I said, "I hear you saying you'd like more time. Let me see if I can arrange extra sessions." When Ron came in the next time, his stance was more sure and his step more firm. "I've been feeling strong, very good. . . . It's as if the metal core that runs through me was all full of holes and fragile. When you heard my need and responded to it, your being in touch with me fused all the holes and made the core solid."

The holes in Ron's core did not get fused together once and for all in a single magical moment, but he was pointing to an important part of the process that he felt could bring solidity to his selfhood. Where did these holes come from? He talked often of his early childhood as a time when he felt not quite seen or heard in the family. A typical statement that expressed his experience of it was, "I can see my mother in the kitchen. She's always there, but her back is always turned."

If you have become dependent on a particular person to make you feel you exist, then you are paying a high emotional price even when the relationship is at its best. But when the relationship is an unhappy one (and most likely it will be if it has to carry the burden of your existence) and you have to face the possibility of its ending, it will feel as if your existence is at stake. In *I'm Dancing as Fast as I Can*, Barbara Gordon writes:

> I was trying to hold on to all the memories of the weekend. But I thought mostly of Jim and I tried to remember every moment of our time together to make it last. But it was over. It was already a memory. How had so many hours of planning and anticipation been relegated so quickly to history? I began to feel hollow, to feel more unreal, the brief fragment of connection I had experienced with him was gone. *I was invisible.**

To break a relationship with someone on whom your sense of existence has depended means that you will have to, sooner or later, risk facing the terror of your own feelings of invisibility and nonexistence. Norma, a woman of forty, had ended her marriage, and several years later she was still so terrified of being alone that she never spent a weekend without the company of a man for at least a substantial part of the time, even if it meant remaining in relationships that were dreadful. And she went from one dreadful relationship to another because she would clutch onto someone new, with little regard for his suitability, to enable her to leave the last disastrous affair. Norma was one of that group of four women I had mentioned before who banded together to help each other with attachment difficulties. The other three all urged and encouraged her to spend one weekend alone, just so she could find out what it was that she was so desperately trying to avoid. They pointed out that even her getting married at eighteen to her first boyfriend had been motivated largely by this fear. With great courage, she decided to do it, despite much anxiety. Her friends suggested that she let herself experience all her feelings, even if they became pretty awful, and try to write down her thoughts and emotions as she was

* Barbara Gordon, *I'm Dancing as Fast as I Can* (N.Y.: Harper & Row, 1979). (Emphasis added.)

going through these "withdrawal symptoms." They also told her that they were available for her to call them. The following week Norma told them her days and nights were so agonizing that at times she actually sat in her apartment howling. Then she read what she had written while in the midst of her fear and pain. Here is a portion of it:

> When I don't have a connection with anyone, I feel like I'm floating, like I'm not attached, like I'm hovering over land, aimlessly drifting this way and that, terrified, wanting to touch, to make contact. . . .
>
> Somebody come! Somebody come! Take care of me. Pay attention to me. Look at me. Do what I need. Hold me. Tune in to me. I'm thinking this but making sounds like a terrified infant! I *am* a terrified infant! . . .
>
> Don't know what to do. Loose! Loose, unmoored. Unattached. Unconnected to anything. Can't see to write. Too many tears. Can hardly hold the pen, can hardly see the paper.
>
> Fear, aloneness. Nobody cares. I could die and no one would care. Alone. Terrified. There isn't anybody anyplace who cares about me. Never was. Not in the way that I need. I need it. I'm so scared. So alone. So unmoored.
>
> Floating, floating. I must touch. Somewhere, something. I can't be this way, unattached isn't even the word. No connection. I will just float off into space. . . .
>
> I will do anything to end this. I will do anything to get them with me. To notice me. To care for me. I need her.* I feel like nothing. I am afraid I will become noth-

* Norma was surprised when she wrote "I need *her*" when she was suffering from being without a *man*, but it confirmed the Attachment Hunger level of her fear of the loss of connection to her mother.

ing. I will just float away. My self, my body will disintegrate. Somebody be there. Somebody come! Please please please please.

For the first time, ever, Norma had faced this terror, this part of her Attachment Hunger that had ruled her life. And painful as it was, she found that she could survive it, that she had all kinds of resources—strength, courage, determination, and a wide variety of interests—and that these qualities gave her a sense of substantial existence. That memorable weekend was so powerful an experience that although her fear would at times rise up, she did not again allow her panic to drive her into a destructive relationship but was free to choose one based on other needs, inclinations, and attractions.

Sooner or later you will have to face your own terror of being without the relationship you know you should end, and that terror may be in part a terror of nonexistence. But it is important to note that Norma did not just suddenly decide, "I'm going to spend the weekend alone and see what happens." With so much unrecognized fear, it was unlikely that she would have made the decision without a lot of groundwork first. And what was this groundwork? Through her supportive group of friends and through personal psychotherapy, she had come to recognize the addictive nature of her relationships. She could see that her need to form an attachment was compulsive and that this need caused her to cling to a relationship even if it was doing bad things to her. She also had come to understand the roots of her Attachment Hunger and how it had been intensified by the death of her adoring father when she was quite young and by having a mother who lacked the capacity to be nurturing and supportive. So Norma knew that what she was afraid of was the re-experiencing of frightening early feelings. All this prepared her for understanding how important it was finally to come face to face with her fears of nonexistence and to discover that she could cope with them. She knew if she could do this, she had a chance of liberating herself from her old patterns and breaking her addiction.

The Value of Friends

Norma had had help from her therapy and her group of friends in getting to that point, but it is very possible to arrive there yourself by recognizing that you are addicted, by seeing what it is doing to your life, and by understanding the nature of how Attachment Hunger and its distortions operate in you. But when it comes to actually taking the step of going cold turkey, particularly when a terror of nonexistence underlies your addiction, you may need the help of others just as the alcoholic or drug addict may need help in withdrawing. Norma chose not to call upon any of her group members as she went through her torment, but she knew she could if she wanted to, that they were there, that they were 100 percent on the side of her effort to face down her addiction, and that they knew how difficult it could be. So their "presence" helped sustain her. And if you are going to face your own monsters by breaking an addiction to a person, it can be enormously helpful to have your own "group" to give you backing. It doesn't have to be a formal group. Again, a few friends who understand what you are trying to do, singly or together, who can empathize with your struggle and who are committed to being an ally to your efforts can make all the difference. Just as we have seen how friends can help when infant time takes over, or when there is a tendency to forget the reasons for wanting to end a relationship, a friend or a network of friends can affirm that you exist, can confirm that you are visible, and can anchor you when you feel you are floating off. (See chapter 16 for more detail on how you can help your friends help you.)

5

YOU ARE
MY MIRROR

"Just as some people use others as a kind of mirror to reassure them that they exist, so others use people upon whom they depend as a mirror to define them, to tell them who they are."* With these words, Althea Horner describes one of the pitfalls that can trip and destroy a good relationship. And it can also be one of the reasons for clinging to a bad relationship. This dependence on another person to tell you who you are, to delineate and even create your identity, can make you feel that to lose that other person is to lose your Self. Listen to Eileen, speaking after one of the several times she stopped seeing Peter but before she could break off with him completely:

* Althea Horner, *Being and Loving* (N.Y.: Schocken, 1978), p. 17.

When I was with Peter I felt I knew my own mind. But now that we've split I can't even decide what to order from a menu. Did I take my cues from him? I don't know what I want, who I am, or who I am supposed to be. I can do my job and be with people, but it doesn't feel like there's a "me" doing it.

Eileen knows that she exists, but her sense of personal identity is very shaky, and for many years she had taken her identity from the relationship she had with Peter. How does it happen that a mature person who is able to carry on a life and to function effectively can still have such a vague sense of who he or she is?

The experience of having a personal identity, just as with your sense of your existence and your trust in your capacity to survive, also has early beginnings. To the extent your parents responded to you as the particular individual you were rather than as "a child" or "their child" or as an extension of themselves, they helped you to become aware of your own unique personhood. You came to feel not only "I am" but "this is who I am." This does not mean that their response is the sole source of your identity. Besides being affected by the reactions of other people, you developed much of the sense of your "me-ness" through your experience of your own body—its boundaries, its capacities, its limitations—and the energy and feelings that course through it. And your inner life—your imagination, ideas, and thought processes—was also a source of identity feelings. But your sense of who you are was shaped primarily by the people closest to you in your earliest years. For example, responses like this would help you to define yourself:

I know you're feeling angry (afraid, excited, etc.).

My, look how strong you are.

Hello, blue eyes.

You have a cute button nose.

You really love to eat.

Other kinds of parental responses may also tend to define you, but according to your parents' needs, feelings, and value judgments:

You're a good (bad) boy.

You break everything you touch.

You'd lose your head if it wasn't attached to you.

If you feel that your sense of identity is precarious, it can be helpful to look at what kind of mirrors your parents were in reflecting you back to yourself. There are several kinds of identity impairments that can be caused by poor mirroring. One is if your feelings about who you are are vague and amorphous. It is what some people mean when they say, "I have no personality." It is a feeling of being a nonidentity or nonentity.

If this feels true for you, it might well indicate that your parents were a dim and cloudy mirror, giving you a poorly defined view of yourself, little feedback, and minimal responsiveness. This would most likely come about if your parents were particularly depressed, withdrawn, preoccupied, detached, or just not around much during your early years.

You may experience an identity impairment of a second kind. You may feel that in yourself you are not a whole person, that you are not *complete* unless you are part of someone else. If that is true, then your parents were probably not a clouded mirror but a distorting one, a mirror that was bent by their need to see you as an extension of themselves or as how they wanted to see you rather than to reflect back your true self. This might have been manifested in statements like:

You're Daddy's little girl.

You can't be afraid of the dark. See, I'm not.

You're Mother's little helper.

You'll never learn how to swim—I'm afraid of the water.

You can't do a thing without me.

Probably everyone has heard his parents say things like this sometime, but if you have a problem feeling yourself to be a complete person rather than as an appendage of someone else or an extension of their wishes, then the chances are that your parents were not as helpful as they might have been in mirroring your *individuality*. And you could have used all the help you could get because when you were an infant your original sense of who you were included your mother or her surrogate. You, as the individual you now know yourself to be, were only a part of that larger entity. Now, to the extent that you successfully achieved a sense of being a separate and whole individual apart from that mother-child matrix, you will feel complete within yourself. But if you never fully achieved this, your feeling of *wholeness* will depend on linking yourself to another person. For most adults, that other person is no longer mother; you may have achieved a break from feeling that she and you are one a long time ago.* But if there are unrepaired feelings of incompleteness, you may have transferred your quest for completion to someone else. And then, when you are without this person or think of breaking with him or her, you can regress to terrible feelings of emptiness. As one long-married man put it, "I used to call her my better half. Well, now I don't feel she is the

* At times, too strong and restricting a tie to your parents may continue into your adulthood. If this is true for you, I would suggest my book, *Cutting Loose: An Adult Guide to Coming to Terms with Your Parents* (N.Y.: Simon & Schuster, 1977, hardcover; Bantam, 1978, paperback).

better half. But even though there's nothing between us but silence and hatred, if I think of actually leaving her, I feel I'd be wrenching away half of myself. I don't know if it would be the right half, left half, top half, bottom half, or more likely my insides, but something would be missing."

There is enormous variation from one person to another in their sense of "me-ness." At a far extreme, I think of a man I tested psychologically during my internship in a psychiatric hospital. As part of the test battery, I asked him to draw a person. He picked up his pencil and drew a nose in the lower left corner of the paper. Then, concentrating very intensely, he followed with an eye in the upper right-hand corner, and then a foot in the middle of the page. He was telling me, with what degree of conscious deliberateness I will never know, how horrifyingly disjointed and fragmented his sense of self was.

At the other extreme are those people with such a keen sense of who they are that they can maintain it in many different situations, roles, and relationships. Most fall between these extremes and may feel somewhat shaky about who they are depending on the situation. And many, like Eileen, gain their identity through having someone else define them. When Peter would say, "You're my woman" or "You're a sharp cookie" or "You're sexy," Eileen would be infused with that identity. When he would say, "You're a bitch, and I won't take that kind of treatment from you," she knew where her boundaries were. And it wasn't just in what he would say. She defined herself as his woman. She defined herself as bad when he was angry and good when he was pleased. She defined herself as attractive when he was sexually responsive and as unattractive when he was disinterested. Depending on his reactions, she would look in the mirror and clearly see herself as beautiful or look in the same mirror and see only a nose that was too big, breasts that were too small, and thighs that were too fat.

Now, with the relationship ended, she felt formless and disorganized. And, while she was not psychotic like the man who made the disconnected figure drawing, she sometimes feared "falling apart" or "having a nervous breakdown" with Peter out of her life.

The feelings of shapelessness, amorphousness, or falling apart are deep rooted, but even though they have early origins they are not fixed in cement. You can change them. But it will take much hard work. As usual, it must begin with the recognition that your identity impairment comes from that Attachment Hunger level, and as such is a distortion of the current reality of who you are. You are a singular, whole, and definite person who feels, falsely, that you are not. And you will have to find all kinds of ways of telling this to yourself. At first, your attempts may be just hollow words, but through repetition they can become part of who you are. For example, in *I'm Dancing as Fast as I Can*, Barbara Gordon is in a struggle to reclaim her identity: "I began my litany. I am Barbara, daughter of Sally and Lou. I am, I am, I am. The catechism didn't really help. But some day, I thought, I'll walk and talk like everybody else, spontaneous and unrehearsed. Until then I'll do my Hail Barbaras. Eventually, it had to work."

When Eileen was struggling to break her tie to Peter and was terrified because when she felt disconnected from him she felt her sense of "me-ness" slipping away, I gave her a list of incomplete sentences and asked her to complete them. Here are a few of her responses:

I am
Margaret Eileen Simmons
a woman
smart
an editor
a Catholic
reasonably attractive

kind
too fat

I was
Meg
a cute girl with patent leather shoes
an honor student
shy

I will be
a chief editor!?!
a mother
dead

I like best to
sleep late
ski
write feature articles

What I like best about myself is
I'm honest
I try not to hurt people
I have a good sense of humor

I deeply believe
in God
that I can have a good love relationship some day
in fairies

If my relationship with Peter were to end
I would cry a lot and get very drunk
I would find a better relationship sooner or later
I would still be me

Eileen knew the importance of developing and holding onto a sense of who she is, so she worked hard on exercises like this, often making up sentence beginnings and giving herself the task of completing them. They helped her to see that she was a person apart from Peter, which was an important step in freeing herself from her addiction to him. (For a list of incomplete sentences you might wish to complete as an exercise in finding and affirming your identity without the person you are trying to break from, see chapter 17.)

Getting the reactions of people who know you well can also be helpful.

One young man, Ben, shaken by the ending of a long love affair, confessed to his friend, "I feel like a nobody, kind of a wraith who drifts through the streets and has no clear form or purpose. I can't see that I leave a mark on anyone. Maybe it's because I have no mark to leave. Do I? Do you see me as someone definite?" His friend responded, "I sure do." He spoke of many ways Ben had influenced him. "I've always admired the way you can make decisions in business and not look back, while I start thinking 'Maybe I should have, if only I.' At times like that, I try to think of how you would handle it." And he went on to document other ways that both he and his wife saw Ben as a very definite person to whom they had clear-cut reactions. Ben let this sink in, let himself see himself through their eyes, let himself feel what fit and what did not.

Ideally, it would be nice if by this time in your life your sense of your identity was clear and firm. But if you must get some affirmation from the reflected appraisals of others, and most of us do, it is far better to get it from *many* people than to be dependent on it from one person. Any one person may have a distorted view and an axe to grind, and, above all, it can make that one person too important to your sense of self-hood.

6

YOU ARE MY SECURITY BLANKET

Eileen told me:

> Since Peter and I broke up, I get these horrible anx-
> iety attacks. Sometimes I wake up terrified. At other
> times the fear hits me suddenly, like when I leave the
> office to go out for lunch. Or when I go shopping. It's as
> if the whole world has become unsafe. . . . There's a
> kind of nameless danger hovering just out of sight. . . .
> With Peter, even when things were at their worst, I
> never felt anything like this. His being in my life made
> me feel safe. He was my security blanket.

Her security blanket. The very use of the term
points to the childhood origins of one of Eileen's most
urgent needs in that relationship. It is the very young
child in Eileen who is feeling, "In my oneness with
Mother I am protected, I am united with her power, I

have nothing to fear. The world is safe and friendly."* But for Eileen, or for you, if Mother went out of the room and turned out the light, then monsters or things that go bump in the night could emerge. Or if you lost her in a crowded department store, the world was suddenly filled with unfriendly or indifferent strangers. If you have transferred that early situation to the present, then you can feel as overwhelmed by terror as if you are still the frail and shaky toddler, and the person you have been attached to is serving as your protecting parent.

I have heard others besides Eileen call the person they are close to their security blanket. And I have heard people, in the throes of a shakeup in a basic relationship, talk of losing their harbor, their haven, their anchor, their defender, and the rock on which they stand. There are many realistic and appropriate ways that a close relationship can give you a feeling of greater security. (I speak of emotional security, not financial security, although in some situations they may be related.) There may be genuine mutual protection and caretaking. The other person may give you support that builds your self-confidence. And in a shared life, you will probably avoid many anxiety-provoking situations by virtue of the fact that most primary relationships, even very open ones, are to some degree insular and provide a structure that limits individual risk taking. Those are realistic security-enhancing assets that you may find in a basic relationship. But when your best judgment tells you that you should end that relationship, and your anxiety increases drastically when you contemplate ending it, then it is probably a hangover of insecurity from childhood that may be causing you to hold on.

---

* And Peter did in many ways stand for her mother, just as the security blanket stands for a kind of portable mother to the toddler. At other times, Peter stood for a strong and protective father.

Let's take a clear look at the anxious state Eileen was in when she finally ended her relationship with Peter. She was apprehensive about going out and doing things on her own, like shopping for clothes or going to a museum, yet she was jumpy and afraid when she was home. After breaking up with Peter she put two extra locks on her door, although when she and Peter had been dating she had never felt the need for the protection of more locks when she was home alone. Though she was often lonely, she was afraid to date new men and avoided opportunities to meet them. She, who was so verbal, felt suddenly that she'd have nothing to say, that she'd be unbearably uncomfortable. She, who was very free and adventurous in sex with Peter, suddenly felt terribly shy and afraid of exposing her body, a body which now seemed to her very deficient.

Eileen could easily recognize these feelings as a return of old anxieties and inadequacy states. She could recall many fears as a child—of the dark, of burglars, and, worst dread of all, of being called on in class. And she recalled many incidents of painful and mortifying shyness. Her mother was not a particularly sensitive and supportive woman. In fact, one of Eileen's earliest memories—she thinks she was three or four—was when she was hiding in her mother's skirt, pressed against her mother's legs because relatives she had never met were visiting. And she recalled how her mother said sharply, "Stop being a baby," and thrust her out, making her kiss all the visitors. Eileen found that her mother was most pleased with her when she was polite and reflected well on her parents. Eileen's own needs and feelings were of little account. Her father, an officer in the merchant marine, was away frequently. He would arrive home with much fanfare, great excitement, and many presents. He would toss Eileen and her two brothers into the air and tussle with them, but after a day or two of this robust interaction, he would begin to respond to Eileen and her siblings as if they were in his way, interferences in his relaxation. When Eileen would try to regain his attention, he would respond angrily. She would retreat, or, if her brothers would let her, she would play with them. She could recall feeling very anxious and insecure after the incidents. And soon her father would go away again.

By recalling the feelings of her childhood and seeing their similarity to her current feelings, Eileen was able to take another important step in understanding her problem. She could see that she was not insecure *because* she was without Peter but the insecurity was a feeling that she had carried within her for years and had simply used her attachment to Peter to keep her anxiety buried. Therefore she had to stop misdirecting her energies into hopes and schemes for Peter's loving return or on efforts to replace him with another Peter who would calm her anxieties. Instead, she had to focus on developing greater feelings of security *within* herself. And that led her to the most important insight of all. She realized that in choosing men like Peter, and she had done so enough times so that she could see it was no accident, she was selecting someone who, while giving her the illusion that she was safe, was really guaranteed to reinforce her feelings of uncertainty and insecurity. Instead of choosing men who, through emotional support and caring, would help her in the job of developing her own feelings of self-confidence and strength, she was choosing men who stimulated old awful feelings about herself.

This led Eileen to question why she repeated such a self-defeating pattern. And that led to the next important insight—her understanding that she was hooked into an old task, a task left over from the Attachment Hunger and early childhood levels. That unresolved task was to make her unresponsive parents more responsive, her poorly nurturing parents more nurturing, her inadequately supportive parents more supportive. She could see that she was trying to solve her childhood wish of getting her parents to be more what she wanted them to be by picking men who treated her like they did, and then trying to change them. Because she could recognize this pattern as one she had created and perpetuated, she could also see that it was within her power to change it. The whole area of her relationships with men seemed less arbitrary and frightening. Her demoralization began to lift.

This is a good illustration of how understanding your own history can alter your feelings and open up the possibility of dealing with your life from a position of greater inner security. So if one of the reasons you hold onto a bad relationship is that you would feel frightened without it, it is important to ask yourself: Just what is this fear? Where does it come from? I am sure you will find, if you allow yourself to think about it, that it is based on childhood feelings of being too small, helpless, and inadequate to deal with the world's demands and dangers. That may have been an accurate perception of your position then, particularly if your parents were not too good at helping you to develop confidence in your own abilities, but it is hardly realistic now. You will have to reorient yourself to discovering that now you are quite capable of coping independently with life. But you can't do it if you continue to depend on someone who is repeating the same pattern of undermining or failing to support your strengths and self-confidence. So it is important to examine your patterns of relationships to see if something self-destructive is being repeated. (See chapter 15, the section on Relationships Reviewed.) If you review the main traits of personality and character in the people with whom you have had important love relationships, are there similarities? Are there similarities in the traits that you found most appealing and most distressing? And what about the *patterns* of interaction? Who was more often in control, who most determined when and how you spent your time together, who seemed more in love and committed?

What needs of yours were most fulfilled and most dis-appointed? How did these past relationships end? Who ended it? Why? What feelings were you left with? Are the patterns of these past relationships similar to the attachment you now feel you should end? If they are, then it would seem that a self-defeating pattern is present and is being repeated in the current relationship.

If such a pattern does emerge, then the next thing you should look at is your early family relation-ships because chances are you are repeating some un-finished business from that period. Eileen was trying to make uninvolved parents more involved, and to get an elusive father to stay. I have seen people who had a parent who was depressed when they were a child consistently getting involved with depressed lovers and then standing on their heads trying to make them smile. I have seen people with a very self-centered parent choose narcissistic lovers and repeatedly beg them for attention. I have seen people with a mean parent choose cruel lovers and try to make them kind. These patterns are guaranteed to continue the feel-ings of insecurity that spawned them. So it is useful to examine what some of the basic interactions in your family were, exploring such questions as:

Who was the boss?
Did one parent love the other more?
What ways did each of your parents use to get what they wanted from each other and from you?
Did you feel each parent loved you?
Did one parent love you more?
Did you love one parent more?
Which parent made you feel good about yourself?
Which parent made you feel bad about yourself?
How did you try to get love, attention, emotional support?
How did you avoid the anger of each?

59

Use these questions to stimulate your thinking, and ask yourself any other questions that occur to you, to explore as deeply as you can your earliest patterns of interaction. If there are people you can ask about the infant and early years of your life, do so. Then try to relate what you have learned to your later pattern of love relationships and to your current relationship. Are you repeating an early interaction that is making you more insecure yet causing you to keep yourself tied to your lover because of this insecurity? Insight into this connection can be a valuable tool in breaking a bad relationship, but before we discuss what you can do next, let's look at an issue closely related to insecurity, the issue of your self-worth and how it is affected by your relationship.

Valuable vs. Worthless

Many people tend to feel that they are more valuable when they are attached to another person. For many, being attached—even to someone ungiving or destructive to their self-esteem—makes them feel that they are more worthwhile than being without that attachment. To lose that relationship means to be worth less, or to be worthless. As one woman said, "It makes me angry that my self-worth feels dependent on being involved with some Joe Jerk, but it is." And this is not a feeling peculiar to women. Many men feel the same way, that they are less valuable without an attachment to a woman, or a particular woman. If you feel this is true for you, it is important to see that this irrationality has its origins at the Attachment Hunger level. When you were an infant, your mother was the most powerful being in the world, and through your oneness with her you felt omnipotent. That feeling of shared omnipotence can be transferred to a new person, in love relationships, and that often has an almost mystical effect in enhancing your feelings of value and power. A trial lawyer who was very much in love with his wife of many years said, "A long time ago I started this ritual. Just before standing to question a particularly important witness or to make a summation, I picture holding my wife very close. Her arms are around my neck and we're kissing. It's like charging my batteries. I get up feeling like Clarence Darrow."

In that instance, this lawyer was very satisfied with his relationship with his wife and had no thought of ending it, so his fantasy had a constructive effect. By putting himself in touch with the feelings of love between himself and his wife he was, perhaps, also in touch with earlier feelings of receiving love and strength from his closeness with his mother. But seeing another person as a prime source of your power has great hazards, particularly when it entices you to stay in a poor relationship. For example, another man described his feelings this way:

Our marriage had been in deep trouble for months, and it looked like it would end. Louise's attacks on me, and her withdrawal from me, made me feel like dirt, like I had no redeeming qualities whatsoever. I began to believe every critical judgment she made about me. I knew I should get out. Then we had one of those sporadic breakthroughs, and we finally connected again. We made love that Sunday morning for the first time in months. . . . That afternoon I went out to do some repairs on the driveway. I had been putting it off for a long time. I had felt too weak to handle the fifty-pound bags of gravel that sat in the garage, but now I could toss them around as if they were down pillows. . . .

I knew this man had come from a large family where his two exhausted parents worked hard, always worried about money, and seemed overwhelmed and resentful that they had so many more children than they had anticipated. He rarely felt worthwhile or important in his family, so he rarely felt worthwhile or important in himself. He said, "The worst thing was I never felt they *enjoyed* me. I hunger to be enjoyed. And on those occasions when Louise delights in me, I forget how the relationship is destroying me." Similarly, a young woman who did not feel particularly valued or enjoyed as a child (except for getting good grades) said:

> I knew that Harry and I had to break it off. There was no way he would leave his wife and kids. And on this particular Monday, which would have been the anniversary of our meeting, I was feeling so worthless that I even said 'excuse me' to a waiter who spilled coffee on me. Then I got home and there was a letter from Harry telling me that though we can't make a life together, he will always love me more than anyone. And even though nothing had changed, objectively, my feelings about myself changed instantly. I looked into the mirror, and I saw a very beautiful woman.

These examples illustrate that the feelings of self-esteem and worthlessness are different sides of the same Attachment Hunger coin and indicate how quickly these judgments about ourselves can change depending on the presence or absence of that basic connection. But it is important to note all three of these people had the capacity within themselves to feel they were terrific, and that the attachment to the other person only activated their capacity to feel it. The lawyer carried within himself the ability to feel like Clarence Darrow, the woman had the capacity to see her own beauty, and the married man obviously always had it in him to toss the bags of gravel. When this truth is recognized, it can be the beginning of important changes.

The man who clung so unhappily to Louise for the moments of feeling valuable and strong he gained when she sporadically "enjoyed" him came to realize that he was seeking fulfillment of an old hunger. He was doing it by trying to extract that feeling of being enjoyed from someone who rarely felt that way about him, and he began to realize that he was involved in a futile and draining task from his own past. At one point he said:

> If it's important to me to feel enjoyed, then that's what I need and want, so I'd better look for someone who really enjoys me. But the thing is, I'm beginning to see that I have a lot on the ball whether there is someone like that or not. I really am strong. Louise didn't give me the strength to toss that gravel. Or to run a successful business. I have to try to hold onto that truth.

And he did struggle to hold onto that truth, by deepening his understanding of how he came to depend on an attachment to make him feel valuable. He did this largely by writing to himself, in the form of a journal, his discoveries about his self-worth, and by forcing himself to read what he wrote when he felt most worthless. Even so, it was months before he felt on firm ground about separating from Louise. (In this instance, even before he could announce his intent to separate, Louise sensed a shift in him. She could feel that he was no longer dependent on her for his self-esteem, and, whether through fear of his leaving or because his new self-regard made him more attractive, she began to shift her response to him. He decided to stay, enjoying being enjoyed more, but no longer feeling tied to her by his old need. This turn of events is not uncommon, but note that it came about not because of a maneuver or "game" but because he really no longer needed her to feel good about himself.)

If you are deriving your feelings of security or worth from a relationship that is making you unhappy, then it will be helpful for you to explore the origins of your underlying feelings of insecurity or poor self-esteem. The object of this is (a) to discover that these shaping experiences no longer pertain as far as a realistic current definition of yourself (As one woman said, "Just because my parents didn't take me seriously doesn't mean I'm not to be taken seriously"), and (b) to determine whether you are choosing relationships and patterns of interaction that are repeating an old and futile drama. In other words, *the aim of this self-exploration is to help you put the past in the past and the present in the present.* This awareness may not be enough for you to take the step of breaking a bad relationship. It will still take personal courage, resolve, and, often, the help of friends as a source of support, perspective, and affirmation of your worth as you move from insight to taking action to break your addictive tie.

7

PEAKS
AND VALLEYS

"I like to think of myself as a stable person," Eileen said,

> but when it comes to Peter, my emotions are about as stable as a roller coaster ride. I can go from the peak of joy to the bleakest depression, and then, if he presses the right buttons, it's up into the clouds again. And I can plunge from the heights of loving feeling to rage— even to murderous hatred. I can't stand the way my feelings are in his hands.

This kind of emotional roller coaster is common in a troubled love relationship. Positive emotions, like joy, trust, and love, may alternate, sometimes rapidly, with disturbing emotions such as depression, jealousy, and hate. When these feelings are so extreme and so changeable, it is an almost certain sign that the Attachment

Hunger level is playing a large part in your involvement, which means that your relationship may well be an addiction. Let's see how this operates in three different emotional dimensions: Love vs. Hate, Trust vs. Jealousy, and Joy vs. Depression.

Love vs. Hate

There are two main reasons that loving feelings can turn instantly into hate when Attachment Hunger is a major component in the relationship. One reason is exemplified by a bit of dialogue between Bob and his friend Jeff:

BOB: I've decided to tell Phyllis I want us to get together again and try to work it out.

JEFF: Why?

BOB: I love her a lot. She's really a wonderful woman. Maybe I gave her too hard a time. Now I feel I can be really loving, and I can make it up to her.

JEFF: What if she doesn't want to come back to you?

BOB: Then I'd want to kill the bitch.

In a flash, Bob went from loving to murderous hate, just at the thought of his not getting what he wanted. Attachment Hunger was operating and, arising as it does in infantile experience, it wanted immediate compliance with its demands. Frustration of these demands can cause fury in the infant and in the Attachment Hungry adult. Bob does not really see Phyllis as a separate being but as an extension of his wishes, and rage at her noncompliance with his wishes is as much a part of his connection to her as are his loving feelings.

A second reason for the coexistence of loving and angry feelings in Attachment Hunger is that when a person feels inadequate, incomplete, insecure, and unhappy without a particular other person, he becomes dependent on that other person to make him feel adequate, complete, secure, and happy. If that is how it is with you, then what power you place in another person's hands! And what resentment you must have of that power! Particularly if you feel that this other person uses that power to control or exploit you. In addition, since you may see the other person as having attributes that you lack, you may be consciously or unconsciously envious of this idealized being, and your envy can erupt into anger at any moment. One woman said, "Whereas I'm shy and have trouble talking, Ken is so outgoing and articulate. It's one of the things I love him for. But when we go to a party and he seems so at ease and becomes the center of attention, I can feel myself hating him."

There is a third reason that your feelings can shift so facilely between love and hate when your attachment needs are dominant. At that early level where your Attachment Hunger dwells, your infant self does not have the capacity to feel that the mother who is smiling and nurturing and making you feel good is the same person as the mother who is angry or preoccupied or who goes away and makes you feel so terrible. It is as if there were two different people, the good mother whom you love and the bad mother whom you hate. When the person you are closely involved with hurts or disappoints you and your feelings flip from love to hate, you are responding as if the object of your feelings were two different people. I remember a child patient, a seven-year-old boy, who literally experienced his mother as one person when she was smiling and another person—"a mean witch"—when she gave vent to her considerable anger. He wanted so much for the witch to die and found it difficult to grasp that she was but one aspect of the same mother. In one session in the playroom I picked up a block that was painted a different color on each side, a block he had played with many times. I faced the blue side toward him and asked, "What color is this block?"

"It's lots of colors."

"But now you can see only blue. Why not call it a blue block?"

"Because I know there's red on the other side, and yellow and white."

"So it's a block of many colors, and right now its blue face is toward you."

"Yes."

"And your mother has many faces, too, and sometimes the smiling face is toward you and sometimes the angry face. But they are all parts of the same mother."

The more he grasped this, the more he realized that he could not kill off the witch without killing off the good mother; he would instead have to find a way to come to terms with her complexity.

When you find such volatility in your feelings, it is as if you are reacting to the other person you are attached to from that early place and are not letting yourself realize that the aspects you hate are part of the whole block, and that rather than squander your energies railing against the block to be different, you have to accept or reject the whole multifaceted block as it is. Lorna is a good example of a person having trouble with her dual feelings. She was in a turmoil about whether to marry Dan, the man she had been involved with for over two years and living with for almost a year. Her feelings were on a roller coaster of love and hate that would make her reactions to Dan inexplicably erratic, so that Dan, too, was on a roller coaster, never quite knowing what to expect. She would wake up at times in the middle of the night in a panic and feel, "I've got to end it. I can't stand being with him." She would be cold and hateful to him that morning. But, often, by the afternoon she would start to think of the many things she loved about him—he was kind and considerate, he was emotionally supportive, and they shared many interests—and she would again feel warm and affectionate. When her feelings would turn negative again, as they inevitably did, her thoughts would be, "You're a weakling. You don't really have any ambition. There is nothing that really excites you or that you believe in. You're a loser. I can't stand you." And then she would feel guilty about having such angry feelings toward such a nice guy.

Lorna struggled with her dilemma for a while. At one point I suggested that she write a letter to herself from the "wisest sage in the world," a sage who lived inside her (and everyone), and that she let this sage advise her. She put off doing this for over a month, probably afraid to learn what this sage would tell her. Then she wrote this letter:

Dear Lorna,

There is no doubt that you love Dan. You don't not love him just because you also dislike him. But the things that you don't like really bother you, and they're not all in your head, they're not all because you're afraid of marriage. Dan is kind and affectionate. But he is also passive and rarely takes the initiative. He is afraid to assert himself or to reach for anything. When you first met him, you needed someone like that. You had so little self-confidence and were so afraid of sex that you could only let yourself get involved with a man who was very safe and undemanding. . . . You knew that he would be dependent and that you wouldn't have to compete with other women and risk being rejected. But you've changed. You have more self-confidence, possibly because of the relationship with Dan. But you can't marry him to repay him. Besides, marriage is not just to another person but to a way of living. And now, if you're honest, you will admit that life with him would be much narrower than the life you want. You can see in those moments of hate and contempt the seeds of what, over time, could grow into your predominant feeling toward Dan, driving out love. You cannot marry him feeling that way.

Lorna felt certain she would have to end it. (Not everyone would come to the same conclusion. Each person has to weigh the factors for himself. But their honest judgment as to how it will work out for both people is an important part of the decision.) But despite Lorna's conclusion, her fears of being adrift and without a source of love ("He's been my best friend. I'll feel all alone") as well as enormous guilt ("How can I hurt Dan like that? He loves me so much, and he has always been good to me") kept her from taking action. She became more moody and irritable with him. At this point, she wrote another letter from the wise sage inside her, saying:

> . . . There is no use pretending he won't be very hurt if you end it. He will. But this does not make deciding to marry him right. It will only lead to greater pain later for both of you. And, instead of a quick hurt, it can be a long drawn-out pain. Dan will be as trapped as you, instead of being free to find someone who would love him with less ambivalence. . . .
>
> You would feel different if you could—it would make everything easier—but you can't. So why feel guilty when you know what's best?

It was many more weeks before Lorna could get herself to tell Dan that she couldn't marry him and that they would have to break up. But the main point here is that Lorna had to face whether she could accept Dan the way he is, with what she loved in him and what she disliked. She knew that she could not continue the relationship pretending that the things that bothered her did not bother her or denying the impact this would have on the way they would live, or ignoring what she could foresee would happen to her feelings. By calling on the wise sage within her she was able to make concrete her own best judgment, and this enabled her to resist the Attachment Hunger level pulls to cling to Dan in love and hate or to insist that he be someone other than who he was.

So, if you are in a relationship where you feel

great swings in feelings from love to hatred and anger, you can be sure that your Attachment Hunger level is activated in that you are trying to maintain a relationship without having accepted the other person's complexity. Probably you are hoping to change the other person, which may be, at root, a way of pursuing an old task of trying to turn your unsatisfying parents into gratifying ones. The intensity of this task and the rage that accompanies it can be just as much a part of the addictive tie as the loving feelings. Perhaps you, like Lorna, can profit by calling upon the wise sage in yourself to give you his (or her) judgment as to what your swings in feelings mean for the future of the relationship and what is best for you to do about it.

Trust vs. Jealousy

When a love relationship is going well, it is often characterized by a basic trust, a trust that may have forerunners in the symbiotic period of infancy, and that can make you feel contentment, relaxation, self-satisfaction, even smugness. It has as its foundation the feeling that the other person is really there for you, that he can be counted on, and that he will not act to hurt you or betray you. Its opposite, distrust, may well take the form of jealousy in your contemporary relationship. If you are jealous, you don't need to be told what a tormenting obsession it can be. It is based on the fear that the person you are close to will become so involved with someone else that it will mean anything from having to share his time and affections to his abandoning you for someone else.

There are few people who can have an important and basic relationship, even a relationship based largely on adult-level affection and sharing, who would not be shaken by the threat of displacement and loss. After all, life gives no guarantees, and the possibility of losing a valued person to someone else is real; it happens, and when it does it is one of the most

71

painful experiences a person can have. So some
amount of jealousy falls within the normal range of
adult human concerns. But when emotions from that
early Attachment Hunger level in your life enter the
picture, all these feelings can rise to an excruciating
level. There can be unbearable feelings of humiliation
as if you have not only been found lacking but have
been disqualified as a desirable partner. (This is more
often true and more intense for men than for women,
perhaps because of the double standard and the culturally transmitted dread of being "cuckolded." Men
are particularly vulnerable to feelings that their man-
liness is being mocked and ridiculed by both his partner and his real or imagined rival.) Suspicion can
begin to border on paranoia and rage can reach murderous proportions, if only in fantasy. And your
jealousy can lead you to overvalue your partner and
confuse you as to what you really feel about the relationship and what you want from it.

The theme of jealousy entered into Lorna's relationship with Dan when she had finally decided to
end the relationship. Dan was stunned and devas-
tated. He accused her of "springing" this on him un-
fairly. "You led me to believe everything was fine.
. . . I know you were irritable at times, but everyone
gets that way." He prevailed on her to give it more
time and told her he was sure he could be more of
what she wanted if she let him know what bothered
her. His request for more time felt reasonable to
Lorna, and she decided to remain for a while longer.
But she increasingly came to believe that the relationship would never work. Just as she was most unhappy, Dan began to seem more cheerful. He began to
get home later than usual, and then one night he came
home at 4 A.M. with some obviously hokey alibi. Lorna
was amazed to find that she was very jealous. She
became suspicious of his comings and goings, and became more emotionally focused on him. She became
more sexually responsive than she had been for a long

time. She began to fear that she would lose him, though asking in bewilderment, "How can I be jealous of someone I was just going to leave?" So Lorna hung in there longer, even though she knew, objectively, that the things about Dan that she didn't like and were incompatible to her needs were mostly still there. She had to admit that if he were having an affair, at least it showed some of the initiative she had always hoped he'd take. After a while, as Lorna realized that her jealousy was based on Attachment Hunger level fears of loss and on early childhood rivalries that were causing her to exalt Dan, she began to regain a more realistic view of him and from that vantage point almost welcomed the possibility of his having an affair as a way of her being able to end the relationship more easily and without guilt. As she began to pull back from him again, Dan's fear of losing *her* became intense again, and *he* became jealous, suspicious, and needy.

You can see from Lorna's (and Dan's) mercurial changes in feelings that jealousy is particularly important in the context of interpersonal addiction because it can lead you to *overvalue and therefore remain with a person who is bad for you.* And one of the most important steps you can take in loosening the addiction is becoming aware of how much your jealousy can cause you to elevate your partner and to recognize that *it is possible to feel jealousy toward someone you don't love, whom you don't like, and even toward someone you heartily dislike, if Attachment Hunger and other early feelings are at work.*

Your jealousy-inflated view of the other person, like Lorna's view of Dan, is based on two false Beliefs:

1.   If someone else wants him, he must be better than I think.
2.   If he wants someone else, the other person must be better than I, and I am being dismissed because I am undesirable.

As for the first Belief, the other person may simply have needs and preferences that are different from yours. And as for the second, your desirability cannot be measured by the reactions of any one person; his attractions and tastes are a very individual matter and will have more to do with where he or she is at that point in his life than with your desirability.

People vary in their jealous reactions. The intensity of the jealousy you feel will depend on several factors in your history.*

The Origins of Jealousy. There are two ways that jealousy can be amplified by feelings from the Attachment Hunger level. First of all, these feelings come from a time when your mother was *everything* —your survival, identity, worth, happiness, and well-being. And secondly, it was a time when she was your *one and only* —there was no one else, and it was inconceivable that there could be someone else besides her. Obviously, if these basic feelings are now switched to another person, it makes him all important, and the threat of his rejecting you means utter devastation.

Later developmental factors also play a role. For example, in the period of early childhood known as the oedipal phase, most children feel a rivalry with their parent of the same sex for the exclusive affections of the parent of the opposite sex. This is a normal phase and does not become a lingering problem if parents make two things clear to the child: (1) that they will not threaten or humiliate him for his normal rivalrous wishes and, (2) that since the love they have for each other is strong and is a different kind of love than the love they have for him he need not fear that

---

* It will also depend on two factors within the other person. One of them, the extent to which the other person is of a type that has a particular magnetism for you, your "attachment fetish," will be discussed in chapter 8. The second, the use of deliberate jealousy-provoking maneuvers by the other person, will be discussed in chapter 10.

his rivalrous wishes will make the situation get out of hand. In Lorna's case, her father tended to be very flirtatious with her, often seeming to enjoy her more than her mother. This kept alive her childhood wishes to beat out her mother. She had become so afraid of these wishes that she had reacted by being late to develop interest in relationships with males. She chose Dan largely because she did not rate him as a prize valuable enough to draw envy or rivalry. Later, when she suspected that he was having an affair, her jealous and competitive feelings rose in full force. Lorna's awareness of these origins helped her to dispel her jealousy.

If there are many unresolved vestiges of an oedipal conflict in you, your jealousy will be heightened by your unconscious dread of the repetition of an old defeat by a more powerful and desirable opponent. And, like Lorna, you will be able to cope with this jealousy better if you take the time to think about the possible early origins of these feelings.

Residues of old sibling rivalries may also intensify your jealousy. If you have battled with one or more siblings for the attention and affection of your parents, you may bring the emotion-packed memories of that struggle into the present situation, as if the real or fantasied person you are embattled with is your sibling adversary and the contemporary person in your life is the parent whose favor you and your sibling fought to win. Again, think about your childhood relationships with your brothers or sisters. Was there competition? Is it being repeated in a current jealousy?

How can you be less vulnerable to jealous reactions, particularly if your jealousy is causing you to hold onto someone whom you should really let go? Perhaps the most important step is to be aware that any feeling you have about your partner's being a *one and only* is coming from the Attachment Hunger level (there was a one-and-only mother) and to challenge this feeling with the reality that this is not true in the adult world. There is no such thing as a one-and-only man or woman for you, a one-and-only person you can feel attracted to or with whom you can feel comfortable or who will want you. There are many people with whom you might have a good and exciting relationship. Whether you will find another relationship is up to you. I recall a woman who told me, "I've discovered not simply that I love Donald and he loves me, but that I'm capable of such a relationship. As much as I love Donald, I know now that if I ever lost him, in a year or two I'd have a good love relationship with someone else because *that desire and that capacity to love is in me.*" What is important is to develop trust, not only in another person but in your own ability to form a new love relationship if the current one ends.

Joy vs. Depression

Perhaps no dimension of emotions is more subject to the "roller coaster ride" that Eileen spoke of than the one that runs from joy to depression. When your Attachment Hunger is being satisfied in a relationship, you are likely to feel extremely happy, even euphoric. When it is not, you may sink into despair and depression. These feelings originate from many levels. On the most mature level, a close and caring relationship satisfies needs for companionship and sharing and sexuality that makes it truly a treasure. When it is going well it is very likely to make you feel good, and when there are disappointments, it is very likely to make you feel bad.

In addition to that mature level, on the level of Attachment Hunger, your mother's smiling at you, holding you, and enjoying you made you feel the deepest pleasure. In your current love relationship this pleasure can be brought on with great intensity by even a simple gesture of affection, a loving look, a hug, an especially thoughtful gift.

And just as an interruption of the flow of your

mother's loving attention caused you despair, so can an interruption of your partner's flow of positive feelings currently make you depressed. Since these Attachment Hunger level mood states can be triggered by even small actions on the part of your partner—a harsh tone, a momentary look of anger or disinterest, a failure to remember a special occasion—your shift from joy to depression can be abrupt and devastating.

Anxiety vs. Depression

As great as the emotional swings are *within the ongoing relationship,* they can be even more intense when you are dealing with the possibility or actuality of the relationship *ending.* The unpleasant feelings you may experience when a love relationship turns sour are of two kinds, both resulting from the loss of something that was once extremely gratifying. The first is a chronic state of depression that may come with *remaining* in a relationship long after the joy or even the love has gone out of it. Although this can feel like a living death, it may be giving you some saving gratifications, such as a sense of continuity or even a hope of a return to what it was.

The second type of unhappy feelings may result from *leaving* or thinking of leaving a relationship where the joy and the love have faded. It carries a painful sense of being alone, lost, and utterly hopeless about ever rekindling the relationship. Lorna expressed her feelings this way:

> I was dying in pieces. I knew I no longer was in love with Dan. I would often dread coming home at night. We would talk at the table at the most superficial "how was your day" level. I avoided going to bed till after he was asleep. I was chronically depressed. And yet actually making the move to pick up and go felt like walking into an abyss and seemed more frighteningly depressing than staying.

77

This dilemma is true even when the limerent feelings have somehow survived in a terrible relationship. I think, for example, of a woman whose husband was so persistently cruel and rejecting that she realized that to save her sanity if not her life she would have to leave him. Yet, in those rare moments when he held her affectionately, or even when she fantasied that he would do so, joy and excitement would fill her and would wash away all her negative feelings. "I love him more than anyone or anything, even though I know I can't live with him. As unhappy as I am, the thought of being without him forever makes me feel I have no reason to live."

If your current relationship is making you unhappy much more than it is making you happy, and if you have done as much as you feel you can do to make it better, then you may have to choose between the chronic depression of staying or the frightening depression of leaving. (Some people make the choice of staying but do not get very depressed, dealing with it by lowering their expectations of the relationship and finding other fulfilling sources of gratification.) Actually, you do not know for sure if you will be depressed if you leave, or just how you will feel. You only know that you are *afraid* to leave, perhaps afraid you will be depressed if you leave. For this reason, it is more accurate to say that *the unpleasant alternatives you will have to choose between are continued depression or anxiety.* On what basis can you make such an unappealing choice?

Remaining stuck in a bad relationship deepens your depression, or flattens it into an ongoing bleakness. Depression is often the emotional state that accompanies helplessness and hopelessness. It is a surrender of personal power, a passive waiting for someone else to change things or a resignation to things remaining as they are. To move to terminate the relationship, assuming you feel you have exhausted the possibilities of improving it, will make you feel tense, agitated, and terribly frightened—all signs of anxiety. But, unlike prolonged depression, anxiety is the state that often accompanies change, activity, movement, and risk taking. And it is often short-lived, fading after the step to end it is taken and sustained. In other words, though anxiety feels horrible, it is often a growing pain. If your judgment leads you to a choice that arouses anxiety, as unpleasant as that feeling is, it is always better to choose anxiety over depression.

If you do not feel quite up to ending the relationship, a good intermediate step is to *give yourself a temporary separation from it*, be it a few months or a few weeks, so that you can see what the terrible feelings you are afraid of are, and so that you can get some sense of how you might cope with them. Much can be learned from this kind of temporary separation. Remember, for example, the woman who spent the awful weekend alone and wrote of her terror of feeling that she was floating off into space, unmoored, uncared about and alone. But she discovered she could survive and deal with her anxiety.

Clark is another person who tried a temporary separation. He is a thirty-six-year-old professor of anthropology who was very much in love (and in limerence) with Paula, a thirty-year-old interior designer. Paula loved Clark, too, but they each wanted very different things from life. Clark liked quiet evenings at home, or going out by themselves or with good friends. He wanted to settle down and have children. Paula loved a lot of activity, wanted them to go out almost every night with lots of people and to places with a great deal of excitement. She prized freedom above all, felt that sexual fidelity was oppressive, and that "the biggest mistake my mother made was to have children, and I'm not going to repeat it." After almost a year of trying to convince Paula of the pleasures of his approach to life, Clark decided he would have to stop seeing her despite his fierce attraction and the fun they often shared. He could see that the fun was getting less and the frustrations getting greater. But he could not get himself to say, "It's all over." The anticipated pain and anxiety seemed too formidable. However, he was able to say, "Let's not see each other for a month and see if that changes anything."

At first, the separation was torture for Clark. He spent much of the first weekend alone and cried a great deal. He was ashamed of the crying but later said, "I began to realize that it was strong to cry, because that's how I really felt. And I was crying because I was losing something truly precious to me." He wrote many of his feelings into a log or diary. Here are some excerpts from the early days of the separation:

I hate her so much that if she were here, I think I'd kill her. How can she prefer her discos and her stupid empty freedom to me?

Paula, Paula, Paula. Please call me and tell me you want me, that you want what I want.

I'm not rich, I'm not good looking, and I'm getting bald. Is there any other woman out there who would want to hug this skinny body?

Who is she with now? I'm all alone, but I'll bet she's not. I feel like killing myself when I picture her doing with another man the things we did.

I just dialed her number but hung up after one ring.

I started to get dressed to go to a singles bar, but the thought of that made me even more depressed. So I'll drink myself into oblivion here at home.

Paula, Paula, Paula. Please.

In succeeding days his diary began to show some change:

Wow! I just realized I didn't think of Paula all day at work. Am I getting free?

I can feel that I'm trying to force myself to like this new woman I met at the gym more than I do. Cut it out.

I'm beginning to miss Paula a lot again. But I can tolerate it. . . . I can also see how absolutely wrong she is for me.

I'm just beginning to come to terms with what it means to be alone. I don't like it, but why should I when it's so new? And I'm learning that just wanting something badly and wishing for it won't bring it to me. . . . I'll have to fill the barren spaces myself. I was wanting Paula to bring the excitement into my life, but I'll have to find my own excitement.

There's a dignity about being alone. It's okay. And it doesn't mean I'm all alone. Stan and my brother have been there when I needed them.

After a month, Clark and Paula got together again as prearranged. There was much of the old attraction, and for a few weeks they saw each other almost as frequently as before. But, as Clark said later:

Nothing basic had changed. Paula is Paula, and I am me. So we finally ended it, and it was sad but very nice in a way. We made love a lot that night and went out for brunch in our favorite place, and I bought her a bag of the chocolate-covered nuts she likes as a good-bye present. If we had tried to stay together longer, it would have ended in hatred and bitterness. It's still sad, but it's also okay. It's as if during that month separation my fever broke. And now I can let her go.

So, again, in helping yourself to cope with the extremes of emotions involved in breaking an addictive relationship, if you do not feel ready for a full cold-turkey withdrawal, you might find it helpful to take a temporary separation and allow yourself to experience whatever the feelings are really like in being without this person. If you want to get the most out of it, don't load up every minute of the separation with distractions and people and tasks. Let yourself feel your feelings. Let the fever peak and break. Don't bring the separation to an end as soon as you feel distress. It is important to confront your Attachment Hunger and to discover that you can endure your withdrawal symptoms so that you can restore yourself to a life governed by your truest self-interest rather than by your addiction.

II

THE WORKINGS OF THE ADDICTION

8

THE OBJECT OF MY AFFECTION

For most people, Attachment Hunger doesn't drive them to latch onto just anybody. It is more selective than that. We may feel friendly toward some people and attracted to some people, but they do not necessarily become the object of our Attachment Hunger. Usually, there is some particular quality a person must have to draw and hold our Attachment Hunger. For each of us, that quality is different, but a person who has it becomes for us what I call the Attachment Fetish Person.

I have borrowed the term "fetish" from the literature of sexual disorders, where it refers to some object, like a piece of clothing or a particular part of the body, that is used in some way by the fetishist in order to achieve sexual arousal and gratification. When I use the term Attachment Fetish Person I am not necessarily referring to someone you must have to feel sexual arousal. I mean that there is some quality that the person *must* have in order for your Attachment Hunger to select *that person* for the gratification of your symbiotic needs. Sometimes sexual attraction is a part of it. But there need be no sexual attraction or limerence for a particular person to become the magnet for your Attachment Hunger and thus the object of your addiction.

ATTRIBUTES OF THE ATTACHMENT FETISH PERSON

The particular qualities a person must have to become the object of your attachment needs fall generally into three categories:

1. Physical attributes
2. Personality characteristics
3. The way he is with you.

Physical Attributes

Most people are more likely to be attracted to one physical type than another, and it may not be just a simple sexual attraction. For each of us, certain physical attributes can readily call forth our deep attachment needs. For example, one thirty-year-old man said:

I only get attracted to short women—to slight, petite ones. It's funny, I'm six foot four, and when I go to a singles' party, as soon as I walk in I get those relieved and welcoming smiles from all the tall women there, and then I head for some five foot zero woman. . . . Maybe I feel secure with someone smaller, or maybe I like the way they look up at me or the feeling of being so big and powerful when I hold them. I don't know, it's just that I'm more comfortable with them, and they turn me on.

Clearly, the physical attraction is there, but it seems to rest on a feeling of security and comfort that is more closely related to attachment needs than to sexual appetite alone. This same point is seen in these examples:

Ken has warm furry eyes that make me feel I can snuggle down in them and be warm and safe.

I like voluptuous women with big breasts—you know, the Earth Mother type.

There's something about icy blue eyes that make me feel a man won't let me push him around, and that makes me feel secure and very, very interested.

When I look at her, with that perfect skin and those high cheekbones, and above all when I listen to her voice, so soft, so melodic, I just melt. It's like I melt into her. . . . I want to hold her so close that we become one.

Mel is so frail and sensitive looking, something like Woody Allen. I want to take good care of him, and that lets me feel very close. . . .

I've always been attracted to jocks. . . . It's not just that they have sexy bodies, but I feel protected when I'm with a guy built like that.

In all of these statements, sexual appeal is present, but there is more stress on the gratification of needs from the Attachment Hunger level than the genital level. Fulfilling these needs can add immeasurably to a good relationship or, tragically, can bind someone to an otherwise dreadful relationship.

Personality Characteristics

If you think about the people you've felt closely attached to in a love relationship, the chances are that they have a lot in common. Besides the fact that many may share similar physical attributes, they may have similar personality characteristics. Eve said, "Every man I've really felt drawn to has been, in some way, brilliant. More than that, he has to like ideas, to be able to play with them, and toss them around like bubbles. I'm excited by it. I become like a little child clapping in awe at a juggler or magician." And, as we will see in more detail later, Eve tended to fall into slavish and self-effacing relationships with these men, becoming their helpmate and nursemaid, always to her own disadvantage. Here are some other examples of the impact of personality characteristics on attachment:

Every woman I've been seriously involved with has been very emotional, very intense. Her intensity makes me feel very alive. The only trouble is, they usually have these extreme highs and lows, and after a while it drives me crazy or just exasperates me.

Bernard is so quiet and withdrawn that there are times I feel like I'm starving to death. But that's been true of just about every guy I've liked from junior high school on. I always think I can bring them out.

I have this thing for self-centered women. You know, those sexy looking ones that every man lusts after but who really is just a selfish, bitchy child. I tell myself that with me she'll be different. When will I learn?

I've always been drawn to men with a broken wing or some tragic flaw—you know, a drinking problem, a wife he hates but can't leave because she's helpless, a rebel who can't hold a job. Maybe something about that brings out the maternal in me.

These men and women are talking about the personality characteristics of the Attachment Fetish Persons, the traits that the other must have for them to become involved in a love relationship. In some instances, the very traits that attract are the ones that also doom the relationship to unhappiness. We will soon explore why this may be so.

The Way He Is with You

Some people are fortunate—they are attracted to people who treat them well, like Sharon who, when she was only fifteen, said, "The boys I like are the ones who like me and show it in how they act. They make me feel good. I can't understand some of my friends who like guys who are mean to them. I'd tell those guys to bug off." But others are like Barbara who told me, "Put me down at any cocktail party or singles' bar—or just a room full of men—and I will unerringly head toward the meanest, most narcissistic bastard there. I've always done it, and I just keep doing it. And once I'm attracted, it's as if he owns me. . . . I get just what I deserve."

There are other dimensions to a person's behavior with you beyond whether he is nice or mean:

He makes me laugh a lot, and I love that.

She's reliable. If she says she'll do something, she does it.

He acts like a little boy with me—irresponsible and unreliable. But I must like it because I've always chosen men like that.

She's like all the women I get involved with—self-centered, ungiving, and cold as a statue.

She accepts me the way I am and gives me the space I need. I never get involved with women who crowd me with a lot of demands.

When the qualities that draw you closer are present, either in terms of physical or personality characteristics, or in the way the person relates to you, it can lead to a bond so powerful, so addictive, that even if

89

the relationship is limiting and destructive, you can find it immeasurably difficult to change it or break it. What does the power of this Attachment Fetish Person derive from? What are the roots of this attraction in you?

ORIGINS OF THE ATTACHMENT FETISH

There is a joke about what happened to Myron when he was drafted into the army. He had never eaten food prepared by anyone but his mother. She hadn't liked him to dine at friends' houses ("How do you know how clean their kitchen is?") or at restaurants ("How do you know what they put in the food?"), so Mother's cooking was all he had known all his life. And all his life, Myron had had heartburn. After several days of army food, Myron was seen dashing to the infirmary, his hand clutching his chest, terror in his eyes. "Quick," he screamed, "get me a doctor. I'm dying. The fire has gone out."

Like many jokes, this one carries profound wisdom. If we have known a certain kind of early nurturing relationship, then whether that nurturance was mostly good for us or bad for us, that kind of nurturing connection is profoundly familiar, the kind we are most at home with, the kind we tend to believe that we need to keep us alive—to keep the fire going. This points to what might be called the *transference* origin of our choice of particular Attachment Fetish qualities.

We can see this transference most clearly if we tend to choose someone who has physical attributes of early important figures. Earlier I referred to a tall man who was consistently drawn to short women. He spoke of the comfort and security he felt with them, and attributed it solely to his being sufficiently larger to feel powerful and confident. But both his mother and older sister were very petite women, so perhaps it is more complicated than he thought. Perhaps there is a *transference* level to his attraction, a level in which the short women he chooses now trigger early emotional memories of the comfortable and loving feelings that he experienced as a child from these smallish women. When I suggested this to him, he was able to recognize that in other ways, too, the women he was now attracted to had a familiarity about them. "I found some pictures of my mother and me together when I was a baby, and she was about the age of the women I go out with now; she looks so much like the women I'm most attracted to—not only the size, but the hair color, the hair length, the shape of the face. It's amazing."

When you think about it, it's not really as amazing as all that. The first loving persons in our lives were bound to leave their stamp on our feelings and longings, even if later we lose sight of what early experience shaped the direction of those longings. I have often found that people with strong fetishistic-like attachments to people of certain physical traits or personality traits have had powerful childhood experiences with people who have these same attributes. Usually, the prototypes are their parents, but not always. One woman was always drawn to tall, skinny, gangly men, men who she later realized looked like her older brother who was a protective and loving teenager when she was a little girl. And one man, whose mother was a cold, rather thin, fashion-conscious woman, was later drawn to women who tended to be chubby, fleshy, and warm, like his mother's sister who lived next door and who adored him during his early years. Sometimes, if we become attached primarily to people with certain physical attributes or personality types, it can be hard to find the early model for these people, but often if we think about it, we can.

At times, though, even if we consistently get hooked on certain types, the origin of the qualities that hook us is more complicated than a simple one-to-one transference. The man just mentioned, for example, who was always forming attachments to somewhat obese women can be viewed not only as being attached to women like his chubby aunt, but as being attracted to women *unlike* his thin and ungiving mother. Indeed, many people consistently get deeply involved with people as opposite to their early parental figures as possible. For some it means choosing people of different appearance or accents or attitudes toward life. Others will go so far as to form their closest relationships with people of religious, ethnic, socioeconomic or racial backgrounds dissimilar to their own. For example, there are white men and women who seem incapable of being attached to any but black partners, and blacks who consistently get involved with white partners. And there are Jewish men and women who persistently get involved with non-Jewish partners, and non-Jewish men and women who are repeatedly drawn to Jewish partners. These people tend to form *anti-transference* Attachment Fetishes. In some instances, like the man who prefers women antithetical to his spare and cold mother, it is a moving away from attributes associated with rejection, abuse, disappointment, constriction, or other negative early experiences. But, again, it can be even more complicated. For example, anti-transference attachments can appeal to a man who, as a child, felt *too* attracted or attached to his mother, or to a woman who, as a child, felt *too* attracted or attached to her father. These people may be making these choices not as a rejection of some pain-inducing behavior on their parents' part, but as a rejection or denial of their own early and possibly unconscious impulses. They cannot allow themselves to get too close to people who would stimulate these old feelings, feelings that are unacceptable because they carry forbidden sexual (oedipal) meaning or because they arouse too strong a wish to become as passive and dependent as they were when they were very young. For them, people of a different background feel both more exotic and safe.

The most compelling and self-destructive patterns are evidenced by those who persist in attaching themselves to people who are clearly bad for them. Earlier I wrote of Eve, the woman who became involved with a series of brilliant and verbal men who toss ideas around "like bubbles." Although Eve was a very bright, able, and well-educated woman, she would put herself in a position of such servility, not only in being their research assistant, typist, cook, and confessor, but in a childlike and humbled stance in the everyday little interactions in the relationship. Besides being "brilliant," the men also tended to be quite autocratic, demanding, and controlling, so that she was knocking herself out for someone who considered her attentions his due, treated her disdainfully, and felt very little need to reciprocate. After a while, either he would end the relationship because he was involved with someone else, or Eve would end it in depression and despair.

It is not difficult to see the origins of Eve's Attachment Fetish in her history. Her father was an intelligent, highly articulate professor of biochemistry whom Eve admired and adored. From Eve's early childhood, she discovered that her father loved to play verbal games with her and that he enjoyed it when she could enter into it with sharpness and wit, but she also soon found that he would become resentful and withdrawn if she "topped" him. Eve would "help" him do crossword puzzles when she was quite young, and would edit and type his articles when she was in high school. Eve's mother was more involved in shopping and decorating than in words and ideas and was often a mute spectator to their interplay. Yet Eve's father loved his wife in a tolerant and protective way.

The messages Eve took from her father in this

situation were: (1) to be bright and verbal could make the eyes of a certain man twinkle, and this was the most exciting thing in the world, (2) to assist him in every way was only right because he was a superior being, (3) she had better not move out of this helpmate role by achievements that overshadowed his, and (4) he would probably choose someone else for his primary relationship. These learnings were transferred from her father to others, causing her to overvalue certain men, to undervalue herself, and to set up a series of doomed relationships. (Her awareness of this pattern and its origins marked, as we will see, the first step in changing it.)

Another example of a self-destructive Attachment Fetish is illustrated by Ben, the man who said, "She's like all the women I get involved with—self-centered, ungiving, and cold as a statue." What would make this otherwise reasonable thirty-five-year-old man become drawn to women who give him nothing? It is probably a truism that we all have needs for nurturing and warm stroking, so why would Ben, or anyone, repeatedly get involved with someone who blatantly fails to meet those needs? It becomes more clear when we learn that Ben's mother was a self-indulgent, remote, and unresponsive woman who was more concerned with being dressed fashionably and with the house being clean and color-coordinated than she was about Ben. He described dinners at home as "nightmares of elegance" and said, "She used to dress me as an accessory." Being deprived of warmth, genuine concern, and involvement magnified Ben's Attachment Hunger many times over. You might think he would later become powerfully attracted to nurturing women who could gratify some of these unfulfilled needs. Some people do make that choice and form relationships with others who give them much more than Mother ever did. But Ben, and many others, instead get hooked into the task of trying to make women who are like his mother finally give him what he needs. It is as if he is determined to get warm milk from a beautiful but cold marble statue. "Romantic" literature, myths, and classics are replete with tales of decent and accomplished men who climb glass mountains, slay dragons, prostrate themselves, and wreck their lives in an obsessive attempt to win some icy woman. It is a futile and life-destroying task, and it can be a fatal addiction.

Jeanne is another example of someone persistently drawn to men who are bad for her. She is the one I quoted as saying, "I've always been drawn to men with a broken wing or some tragic flaw. . . . " Her father was a glamorous but terribly passive and ineffectual man who was able to conceal his helplessness beneath inherited wealth and smoking-jacket charm. As a child, Jeanne worshiped him, and as she grew she struggled hard not to see his weakness. But her father kept disappointing her, not being there for her time after time. As the truth of what he was like broke through, she felt betrayed. "I had been idealizing him, creating an illusion, and then suddenly I couldn't any more. Suddenly I saw him as a pathetic loser. It's still painful. All those wasted years of propping him up. What a sad, stupid waste."

While Jeanne saw this aspect of her relationship with her father quite clearly, it was a longer while before she stopped transferring this interaction to other men. It was Jeanne and people like her that I had in mind when I wrote:

I have seen women with weak fathers unerringly and repeatedly select, out of a large number of men who cross through their life space, men who are little boys in basic ways—perhaps alcoholics, drug addicts, love addicts, failures in careers, inept at earning a living, and unable to assert themselves except perhaps in little-boy demandingness, tantrums and sulkiness. . . .*

* Howard Halpern, *Cutting Loose* (N.Y.: Simon & Schuster, 1977; paperback, Bantam, 1978). The excerpts here are from chapter 4, "The Little Man Who Isn't There."

From a very young age, if you are like Jeanne, you learn what your role in the relationship with such a man is to be:

Initially, at least, it is to deny your man's basic weakness, either by blinding yourself to it completely or by seeing it as some cute or some mildly troublesome quirk. Then when your face or your rear end is sufficiently bruised from falling on one or the other every time you thought your man was strong enough to lean on for occasional emotional, moral or practical support, it may gradually dawn on you that there's some pretty basic defect there. This would be a good time to reevaluate the whole relationship, but if you were hooked into a rescue and rehabilitation fantasy with your father, you'll swiftly and unthinkingly don the uniform of whatever rescue mission is called for— nurse, social worker, vocational counselor, benevolent mother, policeman—and begin the soul-grinding process of lifting up, pumping up, propping up, shoring up and giving up; and then, after briefly resting up, return to lifting up, etc.

This type of rescue operation (whether it be a woman rescuing a helpless and ineffectual man or a man rescuing a helpless and ineffectual woman) is usually based on an attempt to resolve an old frustration with that kind of parent. If you find yourself in that role, you know how addicting such a task can be.

What all these examples of self-defeating Attachment Fetishes have in common is that they are a reflection of low self-esteem. Whether it's Eve and her attraction to dazzling verbal swordsmen, Ben's involvement with women who are cold statues, Jeanne's propensity to rescue broken-winged men, or a persistent attraction to unavailable people, or cruel people, or depressed people, or any other fetish type that has built-in futility, the transference assumption it is based on is that if you can make this other person strong and loving, he or she will make you feel complete, adequate, secure, and happy. Which is another way of saying that without this person you feel that you are incomplete, inadequate, insecure, and unhappy. As long as you continue to believe this, you will always be vulnerable to your particular type of self-defeating attachments.

Probably everybody has a tendency to have Attachment Fetishes because all that means is that we are each likely to be drawn consistently to people with certain qualities rather than with other qualities when we seek gratification of our attachment needs. Those qualities are imprinted in our own histories, although the people, incidents, and emotions that stamped them there may long have been forgotten. The existence of these fetishes is not in itself a cause for concern. Most Attachment Fetishes are quite harmless, except that they may tend to rule out close relationships with some otherwise perfectly suitable people. There can be positive value in these fetishes if they lead you to a good and growing relationship, because they can create an interaction of particular beauty and depth of commitment. In fact, where there is a strong Attachment Fetish component to a reasonably compatible relationship, the power of that attraction can form a bond that can hold the partners together in the storms and strains that confront any two humans trying to traverse life with each other. Attachment Fetishes become harmful when there is inevitable failure and defeat (like being drawn to someone's meanness or someone's unavailability), or when the fetish qualities have such magnetic power that they bind you to a relationship that is in other important respects bad for you. And when this happens, you will have to work on reducing the power of those fetishistic qualities so you can be free to form relationships with a wider and more fulfilling range of people.

This is a difficult task, but not an impossible one. For Eve it began with a series of insights. First, she saw that the problem was not merely in her attraction to bright and verbal men—she long knew that predilection and had always talked of it boastfully. But she now saw that they also had to have two other essential qualities—arrogance and unattainability—and that these two qualities, by definition, ruled out a successful and lasting relationship. She saw the similarity of these men to her father—the brightness, articulateness, arrogance, and unavailability (he played with her but belonged to her mother). And, in sum, Eve saw that she was reenacting an old family drama—being Father's helpmate and playmate but never his woman. She never let herself have a man of her own—that was Mother's territory.

Small changes began to follow these insights. Eve was deeply involved with a man who was chief of research for a large computer corporation. He was astute, witty, imperious, and married. But now, instead of fooling herself that this time it would be different, she could see the ultimate rejection that was built into the relationship. She began to resent being at this man's service as she saw, not only that it would lead nowhere, but how much she was limiting and harming herself in this servile arrangement. This pattern began to lose its excitement, began to seem tawdry and suffocating. Finally, on a day before a weekend they were to spend together, when a messenger arrived with a speech he had written that he wanted her to edit for him, she returned the speech with the messenger and with a note saying, "It was fun, but it's not any more. Thanks for everything and good-bye."

Eve continued to find similar men initially attractive but said, "As soon as I smell their arrogance, or their unavailability, or my becoming 'Daddy's little helper,' an alarm bell goes off. At first I had to force myself to use what I knew to keep away from these men. But more recently they just automatically turn me off. I still like brilliant and verbal men, but there are plenty of those who are decent guys and are at least theoretically available." Her relationships took a clear turn for the better.

9

SELF-DELUSION AND ADDICTION

It isn't easy to maintain an addictive relationship in the face of your own unhappiness, pain, and disappointment. To keep yourself hanging in there you may have learned how to fool yourself into believing you are happy, to anesthetize the pain, to gloss over the disappointment.* It is understandable that we would want to delude ourselves about unpleasant realities when our Attachment Hunger is pushing us to hang in there, but that is as dangerous as taking pain killers to block out the warning signs of serious illness. So let's take a searching look at the self-deceptive maneuvers you may be using to keep yourself in a destructive situation.

---
*Sometimes mind-altering chemicals, like alcohol, tranquilizers, anti-depressants, barbiturates, amphetamines, narcotics, etc., are used as opiates and mood changers so that you can continue not to come to terms with the realities of the relationship.

Rationalization

Your Attachment Hunger desperately seeks to maintain the tie no matter how deadly it is, and your thinking processes can often enter into collusion with it, clearing the way for the Attachment Hunger to control your actions. In the first chapter I indicated how rationalization, the technique of giving yourself good reasons that conceal your underlying reasons, can be used at the service of continuing your addiction. I quoted one woman as saying, "It's not that he doesn't love me. He's just afraid of commitment."

In this particular situation it became obvious that this man did not care for her very much and certainly did not love her. All the evidence for this was there for her to see, but she managed to distort the meaning of the evidence (his coolness and distance) rather than to face a painful truth that might lead her to end the relationship. There are instances where this same rationalization may be true: The person about whom it is made may care but be afraid of commitment. In such cases, the rationalization may be used to avoid facing the question, "Does it matter much that he cares but is unable to make a commitment if commitment is what I want?" Whether it would be best for you to stay or go, only you can decide. But you would be in a better position to make an enlightened decision if you at least challenged the rationalization and looked at what the realities are, perhaps with the help of people more objective. A good rule of thumb is to take the other person's frustrating behavior *at face value* rather than to do fancy mental gymnastics to explain it away. Then you can see whether this face-value view of it is acceptable to you. If it is not, you *will* be faced with the choice of living with it, working on it, or leaving it—but at least you will not be deluding yourself.

Idealization

When someone is your Attachment Fetish Person (particularly when there is limerence), it is very easy to distort who he is in a way that plays up his good points and diminishes or obscures his bad points. That can be an innocuous or even somewhat helpful distortion that can serve to grease the wheels of the relationship over the inevitable rough spots. But when you idealize traits that are causing you much difficulty, or if your idealization is blinding you to ways the relationship is being harmful, then this idealization becomes a malignant self-delusion.

One of the most common forms of this malignant idealization, and a mental maneuver that can be done with equal dexterity by men and women, is in misconstruing the other person's inability to be loving, giving, and supportive as evidence of his strength rather than as a crippling weakness. For example, Liz was long involved with Jim, a man who would maintain a stance of granite immovability in the face of her wishes for a more personal, emotional, and involved responsiveness. His oft-repeated phrase was, "I'm not going to baby you." His standard response to the question of whether he loved her was, "If you don't know, I won't tell you." She saw Jim as a strong and self-contained figure and saw herself in contrast as needy and sniveling. "I admire his strength. He's like a rock. He's not needy. I can see where my wanting affection could turn him off." The pain of feeling shut out and deprived continued, but she tried hard to deal with it as being a product of her own "immature dependency."

In time Liz became aware that although many things in Jim's life were going badly and were, in fact, falling apart, he seemed unable to let her in by talking of his pain and discouragement. He became more withdrawn, sullen, and unapproachable. She began to realize that what she had thought was great strength was really a desperate and brittle defense against his own enormous but denied neediness. She could see his hardness with her as a concealment of and disdain for his own vulnerability. Her needs were a great threat to Jim because he had walled off his own needs and wanted no reminders of them. And she had been making excuses for what she could now see as a severe psychological handicap by elevating it into self-reliant strength.

Liz recalled that both of her parents were rather unemotional, practical, aloof people who were terribly guarded against feelings and dependency. "I didn't believe in all that 'Mommy stuff'" her mother had recently told her in discussing Liz's childhood. Liz noticed how similar this was to Jim's saying, "I'm not going to baby you." Liz could not recall one conversation with her father about her feelings, needs, or goals. For most of her life, Liz would refer to her parents as being undemonstrative but reliable pillars of strength, and she always felt that her own emotional needs were shameful weaknesses. In the last few years Liz had become aware of how greatly her parents had limited themselves through this approach to life but only now, when she could see Jim's armored defense against feelings of need and vulnerability, did she realize that her parents were similarly defended. She realized that when she was small and unable to get the emotional nurturance she wanted from them, she assumed that they, in contrast to her, were strong and above being needy. Being unable to see her parents' ungivingness as a limitation, she concluded that there must be something wrong with her. Retracing the history of her relationships in the light of this insight, she saw that she always had elevated very badly impaired, deeply insecure men into something they were not because she misconstrued their seeming unneediness as mature strength. She now had to face how she felt about Jim and what she wanted to do about the relationship free from this idealization of him.

In a similar vein, there are men who idealize women who are flighty, flashy, seductive, erratic, and unreliable as "real women," never letting themselves see the childishness that often underlies this behavior.

These men are always being bewildered about why all that promise of getting so much in the relationship never gets fulfilled. These men may feel frustrated and despairing, but will often feel the problem to be that they are not man enough for such a woman, rather than face that they are locked into a relationship with a limited little girl. Almost any trait or characteristic can be idealized for the purpose of self-delusion.

Unfounded Hope

Like the fabled optimistic little boy who, on receiving as a present a crate of manure, grabbed a shovel and said, "There must be a pony in there somewhere," there are many people who, when they encounter a relationship filled with the distasteful and offensive, search hopefully for signs that there is something better. And sometimes there is. Sometimes the very acceptance of the relationship *as it is* transforms it into something much more positive. Sometimes beneath the exasperating defenses and frustrating games may be a relationship of much worth that you can find through a combination of acceptance and hard, honest, and caring confrontation. At times, indeed, it pays to grab a shovel and start digging. But you also have to know when to stop digging, when to recognize that there is a lot of manure and no pony. For although hope and optimism are never of greater value than in building something as precarious as a good relationship, unfounded hope becomes a delusion that you can use to keep you endlessly in a punishing relationship. I think of a woman who was my patient who had been married for ten years to a man who was given to periodic bouts of rage in which he smashed furniture, terrorized the children, and, on several occasions, beat her badly. After such episodes he would be contrite and several times entered therapy, with her or alone, to work on the problem. But he would stay in treatment for a while, become

convinced he was now fine, and impulsively terminate it, until the next severe rage attack. In one session, about two weeks after he was particularly abusive and had returned to therapy, she said in talking
of him, "When Tom gets better—" I interrupted her to
say, "What if he never gets better?" She was stunned.
"But he has to. He has gone back to his doctor." We
reviewed their history together, and she had to conclude that over the years his angry outbursts had become more rather than less frequent and violent. She
admitted she could see that he really had no desire to
work on his problems but entered therapy after a bad
episode out of transitory guilt and as an appeasement
to her so she wouldn't leave him. In general, if there
had been any changes, they were for the worse. "I
don't want to accept that, although I know it's true.
. . . The whole room is spinning. . . . If I feel he
won't get better, I know what I'll have to do, and I
can't; I'm afraid to."

Most instances of false hope are not quite as
dramatic as this one that stands up in the face of
actual physical abuse, but it is a very common self-
deception that people use to remain in a bad relationship:

If she didn't really love me, she wouldn't keep going
out with me.

He says he never wants to get married, but many
men have said that who are now married.

There are times she admits that she gives me a hard
time and that always gives me hope that she'll stop.

He (she) says he will cut out drinking (gambling,
drugs, being cruel, disappearing, being irresponsible,
working too hard, tuning me out, criticizing me, being
promiscuous, being unsupportive, etc.), and even
though he has said that many times before, this time I
feel he really means it.

105

How do you tell legitimate hope from unfounded hope? By looking carefully and coldly at the facts. Does the other person say he wants things different from what they are? Is he doing anything about it? Do you and he (she) really want the same thing, or might you be distorting that? Are there significant actual changes in the direction that you want? Have you made real efforts to make it better? What was the result of those efforts? How long has it been unsatisfactory? Is there any hard evidence that by giving it more time it is likely to get better?

An objective exploration of these questions may give you some idea whether you are deluding yourself with false hope or sustaining your morale through a difficult period with legitimate optimism based on a realistic appraisal of the facts and potentials. But since this is difficult to do alone, getting the perspectives of other people, providing they have no strong personal biases about your relationship, can be quite helpful.

Maintaining an Illusion

Often the rationalization and idealization we have been examining are themselves part of a network of techniques to maintain an illusion. And the basic illusion, which is itself a distortion of reality, is, "If I can be connected to this one person and make it good, my life will be wonderful, and if I can't, my life will be horrible, empty, and unhappy." It is, as we have seen, based on the unconscious wish to recapture the experience of a blissful connection with Mother in the very early years and/or a special and exciting connection with Father a little later. One young woman's father literally acted as a "magic genie" promising and presenting her with all she asked and by that causing her to believe she could in fact have him. She would duplicate this relationship by getting involved with unavailable men who by their occasional dramatic display of giving allowed her to maintain the illusion that they were fully available. The process of disillusion was long and hard. At one point when she had pinned her dreams for the fulfillment of the illusion on a married man who she hoped, against all the evidence, would leave his wife for her, she had a dream that her boyfriend had died but that just before he did he had given her this huge palace, "like something out of the Arabian Nights." In the dream she went to his funeral. His wife and children were there, and she became painfully aware of the peripheral role she played in his life. It was not difficult for her to see the message of the dream—that her relationship with the man stood for her "magic genie" father, but that this man's primary relationship (and her father's) was with someone else. The dream occurred at a time when she was in the process of giving up her relationship with this man (symbolized by his dying) and, even more importantly, facing the fact that her quest for a relationship that would transform her world into an enchanted garden was itself an illusion.

If you are to stop this particular form of self-deception, you must try to be aware of every time you find yourself thinking that this is the "one and only" person who can make you happy, whom you can really love, who can turn you on sexually, etc. As soon as you bring "one and only" into it, you are not dealing with reality but are trying to recapture old feelings you knew with your one-and-only mother or father. They were your world at a time when that world and your capacity to deal with it independently were very limited. Now your world is bigger and you have the capacity to create and generate your own happiness; and while a satisfying love relationship can be a big part of that happiness, to hold onto the Belief that only an attachment to this one person can make you happy is to hold onto an illusion that will more likely lead to misery. And there are Beliefs that can also support your living an illusion, Beliefs like "It must

107

work out" or "He (she) must love me because I love him so much." You would do yourself a favor to question some of your basic assumptions about relationships in general and the one that's troubling you now in particular, with the aim of dis-illusioning yourself. Doubtless, some illusions add to life, but not the ones that delude you into staying stuck in an unhappy relationship.

10

THE ART
OF STAYING
HOOKED

Since maintaining the connection with the other person is the single-minded goal of your Attachment Hunger, you have probably developed techniques to achieve that aim. The methods you use may be quite unconscious, and they may play anywhere from a very small to a very large part in your interaction with him, but if you look with honesty at the interaction you will be able to discover how you attempt to *control* the relationship so that your attachment needs can be dependably met.

There are five quite common techniques of control:

1. Control through power
2. Control through weakness
3. Control through servitude
4. Control through guilt
5. Control through jealousy

An exploration of these techniques may help you to recognize the methods that you (or your partner) may be using to ensure that you remain hooked.

Control through Power

In a way, this is the most straightforward technique for controlling a relationship in the service of your own needs. In its extreme forms it is the position of the macho male or bitchy female whose basic statement is, "Do it my way or else." And the ultimate or else is, "I will leave you." It is played most effectively by those who believe that their partner needs them more than they need their partner. One of the most blatant examples I can think of is when a man in the early weeks of his marriage was asked by his wife to help with the dishes. He promptly and methodically dropped each plate of their wedding gift china on the floor one by one. Then he said, "If you ever ask me to do that again, I'll walk out the door and you'll never see me." It worked. She never again did ask him for any help with the "woman's work." But there was an emptiness and deadness that seemed to hover over their relationship.

It is important to note that his use of his adult power did not mean that intense dependency needs were not operating in him. It is likely that if his wife had maintained that his position was unacceptable, that she would insist on his help with some domestic chores, and that if he ever tried to bully her again, she would walk out, then perhaps *his* fear of losing *her* would have come surging to the surface. Then both might have discovered that his attachment needs and his wishes to maintain the marriage were as great as hers. But because often the power ploys of someone controlling a relationship in this way are not challenged, neither party gets to learn how great the neediness of the more authoritarian person is. In fact, outside observers often feel that the power-wielding partner doesn't care much for the obviously more dependent partner. And at times this is true. But in working with couples I have seen the dominating partner literally fall to his or her knees begging the other not to leave him when that usually more compliant partner has said, "I've had it."

Suppose *you* are the person using this power technique to control your partner. What would make you (or anyone) need to control another person through the threat of "or else"? Certainly it is not the most mature part of you. It is, rather, the bratty child part of you, the part of you that as a demanding infant screamed and yelled and tyrannized when you didn't get your way or when the Attachment Hunger was ungratified. Perhaps these power maneuvers were firmed up because they worked too well for too long with your parents, or because you modeled yourself after the way one of your parents treated the other or treated you. Perhaps these power maneuvers serve to conceal your own unacceptable dependency, your fears that your own Attachment Hunger would make you weak and vulnerable. I think of a young woman whose relationships were characterized by her need to dominate and to always be right. Quite understandably, the history of her love relationships read like a catalogue of disasters, and she entered psychotherapy in dismay over this pattern. In one session she talked of a big argument she had with her boyfriend over a movie that he had liked and she hadn't. "You can't have liked it," she told him. And as the argument progressed she had said, "The movie was tasteless and so are you," which made him furious. She was aware that she had come on too strongly and destructively. As we explored her reaction, she said, "If he really liked that movie, then we are different." I said, "Then you are really separate people and not one." She agreed, and began to speak of how uncomfortable it is for her to accept the fact that someone she is involved with can have differing feelings, viewpoints, and preferences because she sees those differences as evidence of the intolerable separateness. At one point she said, "If I picture myself as separate, what I see is me as very little, tiny, in a dark tunnel, and I'm wet, and the wind is blowing through the tunnel. I'm cold and alone, and it will be like this forever." She was in touch with and stating that primal fear, springing from the Attachment Hunger level, of the bleak eternal aloneness that the infant experiences at the breaking of the state of fusion with the mother. At another point she said, "I guess if he's separate, it means he could leave me." This young woman was commanding her mother, in the form of her boyfriend, to do what she said, see things the same way she did, and admit she was right in order to maintain the illusion of oneness and avoid the terror of separateness.

If you are in a relationship in which you dominate but with which you are unhappy enough to want to get out of, it may help you to ponder certain questions:

Might there be a connection between your dominating and your wish to end it? Can you really know, admire, respect, and bring out the best in someone you are intimidating? Can you help but have some contempt for someone who permits you to do it? And if you do not really respect your partner, can you sustain loving feelings toward him or her?

What deep needs from the Attachment Hunger level might you be concealing under your tendency to hold the upper hand? If you must control him, does that indicate that you might be afraid of his being independent of you? Are you?

Beneath the domineering, are you afraid of being vulnerable? Of being weak? Of revealing your dependency? Of being known? And, above all, are you afraid of being left?

Are you feeling so guilty about dominating your partner that you feel too responsible for him to dare to leave him?

What do you think would happen if you gave up your power position? Is it worth trying it to see what would happen before you take the step of leaving the relationship?

In addition to exploring these questions, you might think about an old adage to see if it applies to you. The adage says, "Do not make yourself so big; you're really not so small."

Suppose that it is not you who is always trying to have the upper hand but your partner. Very likely his domineering has much to do with why you may be thinking of getting out of the relationship. But perhaps first it would be helpful to explore whether the problem is not just the other person's need to dominate but the way you have been responding to it. If you have been *submitting*, you could well be experiencing the suffocation, depression, anger, and outrage that often accompanies such a self-abnegating role. And the only solution you may feel open to you is to end the relationship. If you have been *competing* with your partner for control of the relationship, you may be tense, battle weary, and beset by bitterness and painful memories of love feelings shattered by the incessant rivalry. Here, too, the only solution you may feel left to you is to end the relationship. Whether your response has been compliant or combative, you have been contributing to the awful decline of caring reciprocity. It would be very useful for you to consider why. Is it because you don't know any other way to deal with your partner's overbearingness? Perhaps. But if you look more deeply you may see that your response may be your way of keeping a connection going in the service of

113

your own Attachment Hunger. If you comply, it may well be out of the fear that if you don't, you will be unloved and abandoned, a horrifying prospect to the infant in you. If you get combative, it may not be simply to prevent submission but may come from your own needs to dominate and may reflect your attempt to maintain a oneness with the other person on your own terms. And the very combat itself—the arguments, the mayhem, the vitriol—can form an intense emotional connection to the other person that the Attachment Hungry infant in you may prize much more than more placid but less stimulating forms of relating.

So, before concluding that the only possible solution is to leave the other person, it may well be worth your while to risk relating to him in a new way. You would refuse to submit to unreasonable domination, nor would you battle for supremacy. You would take a stance that says, "No, I'm not going along with that demand because that would not be true to myself and would not be self-respecting. I am willing to negotiate to try to find something mutually agreeable. But just because I don't give in to what you want doesn't mean I don't love you." One woman so insisted on getting her way that her marriage was in jeopardy. One frequent area of conflict was that her husband repeatedly requested that for one day and one evening of the weekend she make no social engagements for them so that they could have some relaxed time together. But she loved a whirl of social activity and would consistently fill their weekends with appointments. For a while he would go along with her but would simmer with rage. Often he would explode and insist that she call up and break engagements, or he would punish her with sullenness and silence for days. But after a while, his need to maintain a connection through compliance or combat decreased, and he took a position which basically said this to his wife: "Having time to relax is crucial to me. Being in the thick of things socially is very important to you. In respecting my own needs, I am claiming one day and evening of each weekend to myself or to us alone. If you over-book, I will not attend some of the things you plan, and I will give you the choice of which activities you'd most like me to attend with you. I wish I felt the same way that you do about how to spend our weekends because I enjoy doing things that make you happy, but to go along with this would be against some very important needs of mine." He persisted in this position, often against great pressure, and eventually they were able to work it out satisfactorily. Other issues were also dealt with in this way, and soon he found that his obsessive and frightening thoughts of want-ing a divorce began to fade. If his wife had insisted on getting her way despite his stance and continued to act punitively toward him, he might have concluded that leaving her was the best solution.

Some power maneuvers can be frightening. The threat that "If you try to leave me, I will beat you up, get you in trouble, wreck the house, harm the chil-dren, or kill you" has kept many people in a relation-ship they no longer want. Newspapers often carry stories of people who made good their warning that "If you leave me, it will be the last thing you ever do." If that is your situation, it is important to evaluate as carefully as you can whether the threat is empty or serious and, if it is serious, to plan realistic ways of coping with it rather than to permit yourself to be enslaved by it. You might need help with this from your friends and, if need be, from lawyers, social agencies, law enforcement agencies, or whatever backing you need to keep your partner from tyranniz-ing your life and controlling your destiny. Because whether the "or else's" are great and dangerous, or minor and irritating, it is essential that you recognize that your partner's power game is not solitaire—you are playing it with him. His bullying may tap into a vulnerable child part of you, and your partner may seem more frightening than he should be because he has become some terrifying figure from your past. And it may not be fear alone that is causing you to play this dread game, but the fear may combine with your own Attachment Hunger to keep you paralyzed and locked in. To make any changes, you will have to be honest with yourself about the question, "Am I staying only because I'm scared, or does my fear mask my Attachment Hungry infant's reluctance to break this tie?"

Control through Weakness

Some people can wield their weakness as coercively as another may wield a club. Their basic manifesto is, "I am weak, helpless, dependent, and will fall apart without you. Therefore, you must take care of me, do what I want you to do, be my reliable rock, and never leave me." Some weakness! It is a dominating position that can manipulate someone so effectively that we may wonder why anyone who is commanding through feebleness would want to end the relationship. But if you are using inadequacy and ineffectiveness to keep the other person connected to you, then you know some of the reasons that you may want to break that tie. First of all, it may not be working. Your partner may have gotten tired of the protector role and may have turned off his feelings toward you. And even if he hasn't, you are paying a big price for this maneuver—you have to keep yourself enfeebled and less than a full person. I think of a couple who came to me for counseling at a point when their marriage was in a desperate stage. The wife, Jenny, was a suburban housewife who had avoided learning to drive a car and therefore was dependent on her husband, friends, and neighbors to take her shopping, pick up the children, etc. When the children got sick, hurt, or misbehaved, she would often call her husband at work in a helpless frenzy. She avoided learning anything about the family finances or even changing lightbulbs. Her insulated little world came apart when she discovered that her husband was having an affair. I recall the first session vividly. She sat red-eyed and mousey looking, and her husband seemed weary and contemptuous. At one point when she asked, in effect, what the other woman had that she didn't have, he said, "You're much prettier than she is, you're sweeter than she is, you're even younger than she is. But, dammit, she can stand on her own two feet." As I worked with them, she had a series of self-discoveries. First, she could understand what a drag she was on her husband and others and how unbecoming such helplessness was in an adult woman. She was able to see that she was very similar to her mother in this regard. Jenny also saw that her mother was not only a model for being ineffectual but that in growing up, whenever Jenny was competent and independent, it threatened to break an attachment bond with her mother that was based on their shared incapacity. Her father, in scowling disdain, took charge of all but the most trivial matters in the family. Jenny recognized that in assuming the helpless role she was symbolically remaining tied to her mother and was recreating her parent's marriage in her own. She saw that she was trying to hold onto her husband by being more his little girl than his equal. This prompted her to begin to face her lifelong fears and inhibitions about being strong and capable. She said to her husband, "I'm not that helpless. After all, it was me who took the initiative to find us a therapist and to get you to come here."

Being helpless and dependent, even when it seems to work to fulfill your Attachment Hunger need to leash the other person to you, is very costly to your self-esteem. You can place yourself in the double bind of coming to hate the partner you are so dependent upon, yet feeling incapable of leaving him because of that dependence. In controlling through weakness, as with all addictive maneuvers, the primary issue is not

117

breaking with your partner but stopping this destructive maneuver. If you can do that, you would be less under the sway of your Attachment Hunger, and you could either improve the relationship or end it if that seems best.

If your partner is controlling you through weakness, you know how easily you can fall into believing that the other person's self-esteem, sense of existence, even his survival depends on you. So even though his dependence is choking you, how can you dare to leave him? One woman, referring to her husband's seeming fragility, said, "I feel he's like one of those animal figures in *The Glass Menagerie*. I have to be careful or he'll break . . . and if I leave him, I'm afraid he'll shatter to bits." But your partner is not that fragile and helpless. He made it in this world before you were in his life, and he can if you are out of his life. If you won't let his dependency control you, you may not want to leave him. But you need not remain there because you buy the myth that he can function only with your help and support.

Control through Servitude

In the example I gave of the couple who came for counseling, we looked at how this wife, through her attempt to control through weakness, learned how she contributed to the mess their marriage was in. But her husband, too, had much to learn. At first he assumed the burdened mien of a man who had burned himself out in the unwelcome but unavoidable task of taking care of his ineffectual wife. But when I focused on why he went along with this role, he was, in time, able to see that this position met many of his own needs as well. He had profound doubts as to whether anyone could consistently love him, and he took a role of reliable servitude to avoid the rejection he dreaded. We were able to see that despite his complaints about his wife's helplessness, he had a big stake in keeping her dependent. He also came to understand how his self-doubts arose in his relationship with parents who were hard-working, dedicated but emotionally constricted people. Getting affectionate responses from them was difficult, but he learned early that they valued hard work and service and that he could feel loved and accepted by being helpful. By transferring this pattern to his marriage, both by choosing a woman who felt dependent and then by putting her on his shoulders, he could feel secure that his wife's helplessness would keep her from ever leaving him. But he was getting more and more irritated and resentful of carrying her and finding himself increasingly attracted to women who seemed more resourceful.

If servitude is your game, it is important to recognize how it serves your Attachment Hunger by proclaiming, "I will make myself so useful, so indispensable that you will be bound to me and you will be unable to leave me." And then you have to ask yourself, "Is 'being of service' really all I have to offer? Where did I get that idea? What needs of mine am I denying, what aspects of me am I doing violence to, by playing this unctuous role?" And most important question of all, "Do I dare to stop being the ever-ready helpmate, servant, secretary, cheerleader, etc., and thus risk discovering if I can be valued, loved, and unabandoned even if I am not being 'useful?'"

If you are the *object* of your partner's servitude, you also have some questions to face. You might wonder if his (her) being of service has anything to do with your dissatisfaction with the relationship. I remember one man who said, "It's confusing. I love *it* ('it' being his wife's efficient and consistent meeting of his needs), but I hate *her* for doing *it*." That is often the feeling—it's nice to be well taken care of, it is convenient, helpful, and secure—but if you sense that the other person is doing it through a disregard and denial of his or her own needs, autonomy, and growth, it is easy to develop a disdain that turns off feelings of respect and romance. Yet you may participate in this love-destroying interaction not only because being well served has some inviting advantages, but because it recapitulates that blissful "forgotten" time in your infancy and early childhood when you were doted on and were at the center of someone's efforts and energies, and because you may need the security of feeling that anyone who so makes himself an extension of your wishes probably needs you so much that he will never leave you. But liking *it* may be causing you to hate *her* (or *him*) so much that you want to leave. Maybe you ought to stop your end of the master-servant game before you take steps to leave, so you can first see how it goes between you as self-respecting equals.

Control through Guilt

The human mind has probably not devised a more effective technique for one person to manipulate another (outside of outright threat to life and limb) than through provoking guilt. If your parents used guilt provocation to control your behavior, it is both more likely that you will use it (through imitation) and that you will be vulnerable to it (through exposure). In an earlier book I wrote of the impact of the "martyred mother" whose efforts to control her child take the form of making him feel that he is the cause of all her unhappiness, anxiety, illness, and even imminent death, and I noted that she is effective because she starts early, when the child desperately wants to keep her from being distressed because his own security depends on it. If this was your lot, then it created a weak spot in you, a private parcel of guilt that "is filled with all the things you ever did or thought that you felt were wrong. It contains some of your shameful secrets. But, above all, it contains all your early training that to want, do, or be something that Mother would not approve of will upset her, and that you, as the cause of this upset, are therefore bad. Not only have you received the message, 'Do what I want and I'll love you; don't do what I want and I won't love you'—an injunction of enormous power to the dependent child—but martyred Mother has added another message: 'If you don't do what I want, it makes me suffer and you are selfish and hurtful.' These messages, striking at the dependency and guilt of your inner child, put termites in the underpinnings of your selfhood.''*

In a love relationship, the guilt provocation may take many forms. Often it is subtle and unspoken—a pained look, a sigh, tears brimming the eyelid, silence. But it is spoken, sometimes in words so trite that it sounds like satire to recount them, but these words can be deadly in the real situation. See if some of these are familiar:

You were too busy to remember my birthday?

I could have really made it in my career if you didn't insist on our having children right away.

Of course I get sick all the time, but I bet I wouldn't if we made love more often.

You knew I had a job interview, but you never called to wish me luck.

If you were nicer to me, maybe I wouldn't have to drink.

I work hard all day, and you can't even have the dinner ready on time.

Stop yelling at me. I'm getting those chest pains again.

You go have a good time. We never do anything together anyhow.

* Howard Halpern, *Cutting Loose: An Adult Guide to Coming to Terms with Your Parents* (N.Y.: Simon & Schuster, 1977, p. 53; Bantam paperback edition, 1978, p. 40).

If you had been willing to relocate, I'd be a vice-president by now.

If you cared, you wouldn't have kept me waiting in the rain. I'll probably get pneumonia.

I'm glad at least one of us is happy with the vacation plans.

Of course the kids have problems. You never spend time with them.

Everyone else called to find out how my father's operation went.

The doctor said you're giving me a nervous breakdown.

Just about everyone has been the sender or receiver of such messages from time to time, but when they are a consistent theme in the relationship, they create a motif that says, "I am good and you are bad. I am the victim, and you are the persecutor. And since you hurt me, you now owe it to me to be nice to me." When this theme becomes part of the conflict between your wishes to maintain or to sever a relationship, guilt provocation can be a megaton weapon in the arsenal of Attachment Hunger. The guilt provoker is saying or implying, "If you leave me, I will fall apart (have nothing to live for, be eternally alone and unhappy, curl up and die, kill myself, etc.), and it will be all your fault. After all I've done for you, after all we've shared and planned, after I've depended on you—how can you do this to me?" And even when this is said in the context of an awful, unhappy, destructive relationship, such an indictment can cause the accused partner to hang in there. In fact, it can often hook into his own Attachment Hunger needs, his own fears of leaving, and thus can form a rationalization for staying. In other words, the statement, "I can't be so mean as to hurt him (her) and betray his trust" often conceals the Attachment Hunger feeling: "I'm terrified to make the break."

Frequently, both parties are using guilt provocation—"You think I abuse *you* badly? Look what you did to *me*." It becomes a kind of escalation of accusations, a battle in which, to win, you must be sure to have bloodier wounds than your partner. People can remain together indefinitely in this vicious blame game, but the price is ever-deepening despair. If you are the martyred guilt provoker, you should focus on how you are using guilt to control your partner and be aware of the destructive effect of this technique on each of you. It would be helpful to then ask yourself why you are using such a shoddy manipulation. One woman, confronted with this question, finally came to the conclusion, "The first reason I do it is that my parents did it with me—you know, 'You'll be the death of me.' The second reason I use guilt is that it gives me a hold on Bill, and sometimes I think it's all I have to hold him with."

Perhaps your own guilt provoking has served to sour the relationship for you as well as for your partner because to use it you have to keep yourself in the powerful but unhappy role of victim. It can't get better until you stop yourself from using the tools of the trade—accusing, blaming, getting yourself injured, displaying your wounds, using phrases like "it's all your fault," "if it weren't for you," "look what you've done to me," and other assorted techniques of making your partner feel terrible. Recognizing that you are doing this to control the other person and that it is poisoning the relationship may give you the incentive to stop doing it. But it will not be easy to give it up, because you learned it early, because it can, to a degree, be effective, and because it means taking the risk that the other person will want to be with you, will care about you, and will meet enough of your needs even if you don't make him feel guilty. Stopping your accusations may improve the relationship to a point where you won't want to leave it, but even if it doesn't, you would feel freer to leave it if you chose to because you won't be caught up in this reciprocal exchange of bad feelings that may be making you feel as guilty as your partner.

If it is your partner who is playing "victim" and accusing you of being the persecutor, check out as objectively as you can whether or not you are really being so awful and hurtful. Where possible, ask some friends whose judgment you respect. If they point out things you do that understandably provoke these accusations, you can work on changing such behavior. This would be a lot better than entering the blame game by making countercharges or by being contrite to the point of submission. And the chances are that you are not being as "bad" as your guilt-provoking partner would have you feel. Recognizing this can help you to realize that you don't have to remain in the relationship, if you don't want to, out of a manipulated sense of guilt. And, above all, it is important to realize that your partner doesn't have to fall apart, be forever unhappy, kill himself or whatever. To a great extent, such consequences would be his choice, not an inevitable consequence of your leaving. It could even be, and often is, an opportunity for a new and better life for your partner. So, while there may be good reasons for you to stay in the relationship, being blackmailed by guilt is not one of them.

Control through Jealousy

It is a rare person who cannot be made to feel jealousy. Our vulnerability to jealousy is based on two fears. One is the fear that we will lose the other person, and this can be a terrifying threat to many of our needs, including those on the Attachment Hunger level where the possibility of that loss can feel catastrophic. The second fear is that if our partner becomes involved with someone else, it means that we are no good. We can easily believe that our rival is better than we are—more attractive, appealing, and worthy—for, certainly, if we did not suffer by comparison, why should our partner be interested in this other person? Old feelings of inadequacy and of early unhappy rivalries can be brought to the fore. (See chapter 7 for a more extended discussion of jealousy.)

This vulnerable place makes it possible for your partner to provoke jealousy in you in order to intensify your involvement with him and as a way of getting you to value him more highly, because the arousal of jealousy accomplishes both these things. And your awareness of your partner's vulnerability makes it possible for you to arouse jealousy in him as a way to intensify his involvement with you and value you more. Stimulating jealousy, therefore, can be a powerful but dangerous manipulation in a love relationship. It is dangerous because it arouses feelings that are directly opposite to those that make for a good love relationship: instead of trust there is distrust; instead of tenderness there is rage; instead of friendliness there is vindictiveness; instead of serenity there is turmoil. But my, how effective it can sometimes be. One woman said, "Whenever I feel Joe losing interest, all I have to do is flirt with some other man at a party—or even bring up the name of some old boyfriend." And one man said, "When Bea gets bitchy and ungiving, I just arrange to 'work late' a few nights. I don't even see another woman. She questions me suspiciously, but she sure gets more attentive. And you know what's a dynamite combination? 'Working late' and then bringing home little presents."

Minor jealousy games can be harmless enough, can even heighten the sexuality in the situation because of the stimulating results of what sexologists call the "barrier effect." But there can be disastrous consequences when this maneuver arouses more bad feelings than the people involved can handle (even leading to "crimes of passion") or when it is used to hold onto someone who wants to leave. A woman in

her thirties who was in a stormy relationship for three
years said:

> I know Ira wants out. He tells me as much. And ra-
> tionally I know that if he wants to go, I should let him.
> But I can't stand the thought of it being over, and of
> being rejected. So sometimes I don't answer the phone
> all night or leave matchbooks around from restaurants
> or motels we never went to, and soon he's declaring his
> undying love. If all else fails, I'll remove my diaphragm
> from its case in my medicine cabinet.

And Ira told me:

> I should have ended it with Kate long ago. We're bad
> for each other. And I really don't love her. I don't even
> like her much any more. But when I get these hints
> that she's seeing another man, I go crazy with jealousy.
> I picture them together, doing things we do, wondering
> if she's enjoying it more, if he's better sexually, and
> soon I'm feeling that she's the most beautiful, wonder-
> ful woman in the world, that I may lose this one and
> only perfect treasure if I don't move quickly to keep her
> from slipping away. And once I feel I have her again,
> it's the same old crap.

Ira's words point to some important truths:

> You don't have to love or even like somebody to be
> jealous. (In fact, you can be jealous of someone you
> can't stand.)

> When you are in the throes of jealousy, it can feel like
> you love the other person madly, but this can be an
> illusion.

> When you are in the throes of jealousy, you idealize
> the other person and downgrade your own worth and
> attractiveness.

The "one and only" feelings that often accompany jealousy come from that early childhood Attachment Hunger level when Mother was the most beautiful, wonderful, "one and only" gratifier of your deepest needs.

Jealousy is a highly unreliable guide to whether to stay in a relationship or leave it.

Staying in a relationship primarily because of your own jealousy or through manipulating the jealousy of the other person is a guarantee of unending tension and torment.

The first step in avoiding being trapped by your own jealousy is recognizing the above truths. You can then use this recognition to help yourself in several ways: to stop fooling yourself into thinking that because you are jealous you must be in love, to stop overvaluing your partner and undervaluing yourself when you feel someone else may be in the picture, and to stop letting your Attachment Hungry inner infant panic you into thinking that your partner is the one and only person for you. And you will also have to challenge some culturally assimilated Beliefs you may hold that it is a disgrace and humiliation *for you* if your partner is involved with someone else. That involvement may say much about him and about your relationship with each other, but it is not a measure of your worthiness or appeal.

If you are using jealousy to hold onto someone where you yourself have many misgivings about the relationship, you have to confront your reasons. Is it a need to control your partner? To torture him? To get even? To extort artificial signs of his love? Of his bondage? Is it the Attachment Hungry infant in you who is afraid of the ending of the relationship and so is inducing jealousy in your partner to keep him on a string? Whether you are the jealousy-provoking puppeteer or the jealous puppet, you are at one end of this jaundiced string or another. If you let yourself see the Attachment Hunger distortions and false Beliefs behind these manipulations, you may be able to let go of the string and give yourself the freedom to decide how you, as a self-determining adult, feel about the relationship and about what you want to do about it.

Ending the Phoniness

One thing all these Attachment-Maintaining Maneuvers have in common is their phoniness. Whether the control is through power, weakness, servitude, guilt, or jealousy, authenticity and honesty are driven out of the relationship. If you are using such devices, you may be keeping someone in the relationship with you who doesn't want to be with you and who doesn't love you. Is that really what you want? If someone is using these maneuvers with you, your own vulnerable spots are being exploited to keep you from being yourself and knowing what you want of the relationship. There is plenty of reason for you to regain control from the Attachment Hungry infant inside you who, through using such manipulations or going along with the manipulations of your partner, keeps your addictive tie intact.

11

ATTACHMENT HUNGER: GOOD OR BAD?

When Attachment Hunger rules your feelings and your actions, it can cause powerful bodily and emotional reactions that can override your judgment, distort your perceptions of time and people, and shape your feelings about yourself. It is at the base of your addictive ties to other people. That makes Attachment Hunger seem like a clearly destructive force that you had best try to eliminate. But is Attachment Hunger always destructive? Must you root it out? Does it have no valid place in a relationship?

In chapter 2 I indicated that Attachment Hunger can have positive effects on our emotions and our behavior. I referred to an experiment by Lloyd Silverman (see page 19) in which people with bug phobias had their fear markedly reduced by peering into a tachistoscope where the words *Mommy and I are one* were subliminally flashed. In another study, "two groups of undergraduate college students, matched for academic performance, were given tachistoscope stimulation at the beginning of a law class four times a week over a six-week summer session term. For one group the message subliminally flashed was *Mommy and I are one*, while for their matched counterparts it was the neutral message, *People are walking*. The students in the former group received grades on their final exam (blindly marked) that were significantly and substantially higher than those of the controls (average marks of 90.4 percent and 82.7 percent respectively)."* In other studies reported in the same article the subliminal flashing of the words *Mommy and I are one* had therapeutic and relaxing effects on phobias, obesity, schizophrenic symptomatology, and other emotional disorders. Dr. Silverman hypothesizes that this phrase has such an ameliorating effect on his subjects for several reasons, among them: "magical fulfillment of . . . wishes emanating from the earliest developmental level, particularly wishes for oral gratification and maternal warmth"; insurance that Mother won't leave and abandon them, and a reduction in the threat they experience in temporary separations because, after all, Mommy and I are one; and a fusion with Mother's strength that can magically remedy all shortcomings and impairments (p. 574).

Obviously, Attachment Hunger can influence us in very complex and even contradictory ways. It is at the root of interpersonal addictions that cause us to cling to self-destructive and unhappy relationships, and yet there is evidence of the beneficial effects of

---

* This quotation is from an article by Lloyd Silverman, Ph.D., entitled: "Unconscious Symbiotic Fantasy: A Ubiquitous Therapeutic Agent," published in the *International Journal of Psychoanalytic Psychotherapy*, 1978–79, Volume 7, p. 568. He is here reporting a study by K. Parker called: "The Effects of Subliminal Merging Stimuli on the Academic Performance of College Students," 1977, unpublished doctoral dissertation, New York University.

satisfying our Attachment Hunger. We can either gain a great deal from pursuing the gratification of our primal (and possibly universal) longing to re-experience our "forgotten" state of early oneness with our mother, or we can be destroyed by the quest. This is not really a contradiction. As in many human situations, it is a matter of how we go about things. And, above all, it is a matter of the price that we pay for this gratification that determines whether, overall, its effects will be wholesome or ruinous.

The most common arena in which people seek the gratification of Attachment Hunger is in a love relationship, but it is not the only one. Symbiotic fulfillment is also a profound part of the appeal of most religions. Being "one with God," or taking the blood and body of Jesus into your own body, or feeling the secure certainty that you are loved by a Higher Power all symbolically satisfy aspects of this symbiotic wish.* Religions that stress being at one with the universe and encourage transcendental states stimulate a feeling of attachment to something greater than oneself. So do rituals with long traditions, singing and praying in unison, and the altered consciousness that may come about in chanting, meditation, fasting, whirling, and trance experiences. In their chapter on "The Search for Oneness in the Real World,"† Silverman and his co-authors discuss in some detail the pursuit of this feeling of fusion in religious as well as nonreligious meditation, mind-altering drugs, cult living, and jogging. (They quote one runner as saying, "I felt . . . a peak feeling . . . I

---

* The fact that some of these examples involve male figures suggests that the pursuit of the oneness experience may often be a wish for merger with Father, and that its object is not always Mother or simply transferred from Mother to male figures. Psychodynamic observations of both men and women in psychotherapy certainly support the presence of a frequent and powerful wish for the father-fusion.

† Silverman, et al., *op. cit.*, chapter 6.

131

take the universe around me and wrap myself in it and become one with it."*)

Clearly, all of these pursuits provide some very beneficial effects on those who participate in them, possibly through their gratification of the largely unconscious symbiotic wish. These experiences break through feelings of isolation, lostness, smallness, and vulnerability, and can create feelings of connection, significance, serenity, and strength, feelings that can translate into a robust and harmonious approach to life. But all of these arenas, depending again on how they are pursued and the price that is paid, can also lead to emotional crippling. For example, a person may get great solace and security from his religion through feeling at one with God, his co-religionists, and an ancient tradition. But if this solace is at the price of a greatly narrowed outlook, a lessening of his capacity to think for himself, or a disdain and hatred for people with differing beliefs or behavior, then the cost is very high, and the destructive effects might outweigh the constructive ones. Each person has to weigh that trade-off for himself. We see this in the extreme when religious groups become cults. There is no doubt that Jim Jones met the Attachment Hunger needs of his followers, allowing them to submit to and *unite* with his power, and to be infused with the strength, joy, and harmony of that union. But that same Attachment Hunger connection, in destroying their belief in the judgment and wisdom of their individual selves, led them to surrender to his command to die, perhaps in the pursuit of even a more complete oneness through death.

We could make a similar point about experiences with mind-altering drugs. Many people report cosmic experiences, feelings of the dissolution of their body boundaries, and a sense of merging with the universe

* Sheehan, *Running and Being* (N.Y.: Simon & Schuster, 1978), pp. 227, 229.

in drug-induced states, particularly with hallucinogenic drugs. Others enjoy a sense of bliss, ease, and serenity that may recapture feelings from the early symbiotic stage. Many consider their drug experiences as beneficial and transforming events of their lives. Some participants in an experimental program of LSD therapy count it as the most effective therapy of several other kinds that they had experienced. But obviously when the overuse or careless use of these substances leads to drug dependence, physical deterioration, impairment of thinking, and diminution of the motivation to deal effectively with one's life, the cost dangerously overbalances the Attachment Hunger gratification attained.

Even jogging, which has many emotional and physical benefits, has its hazards, particularly when it is imprudently undertaken or overdone. It can lead to serious orthopedic problems and may even precipitate the very heart attack jogging is supposed to avert. And it can become addictive in its own right. I have seen people become so obsessed with running and so uncomfortable and anxious about missing a planned run that the activity begins to interfere with other important areas of life. Perhaps the altered mental state it produces, the rhythmical movement, the spiritual harmony with all around them that some runners report can provide such a powerful reliving of euphoric feelings (feelings that are similar to the original symbiosis) that the pursuit of this gratifying experience can become an obsession.

In the same way, an important and intimate relationship with another person, because it approximates the one-to-one closeness of the mother-child interaction (it often involves physical intimacy, and there are usually intense emotional connections), can be the most profound and precious way to gratify the need for fusion that most people know. Call it a love relationship, a primary commitment, limerence, or an affectionate familiarity, it has the potential to

133

satisfy longings that arise from many different levels: the practical needs that are better met when people collaborate, the special joys of shared experiencing, the pleasures of mature loving, the self-stretching of caring and nurturing, *and the gratification of Attachment Hunger.* When these Attachment Hunger needs are met, it usually feels good, and most people are likely to experience greater happiness, strength, confidence, and health, provided that the emotional price tag they pay does not outweigh the benefits gained.

If you question whether ending a particular relationship is the best thing for you to do, one of the most important factors for you to consider is whether the cost in terms of self-respect, personal growth, and overall fulfillment is worth the gratification of early attachment needs it provides. How do you determine this often delicate balance? When is the cost too high? How do you know when the cost is so high and so unchangeable that the best thing to do is to break a relationship? Though this decision is a complex and individual matter, there are, as we will see, some guidelines.

12

BUT SHOULD
I END IT?

At times I feel absolutely sure that I should end this relationship. In fact, it often feels like the *only* sensible thing to do. And other times I feel that ending it would be crazy—that there's a lot I get from it that I don't want to throw away. The worst part is not being able to make up my mind.

Deciding whether or not to break a relationship involves factors that are emotionally powerful, very complex, and wholly subjective. There is usually no clear-cut and easily apparent "best thing." As you try to decide, you may feel yourself trapped between two opposite but equally destructive dangers. One is the danger that is inherent in choosing to remain in an unhappy, unhealthy, and limiting relationship. We have discussed that danger in much detail. But it must also be recognized that great damage to both your partner and

and yourself can also be caused by choosing to end a relationship impulsively or prematurely because you have encountered disappointing failures of the relationship to meet your expectations, expectations that may have been unrealistic in the first place.

These opposing hazards make the process of deciding whether to terminate a relationship one which must be made with much patience, soul searching, and honesty—and with a judicious weighing of all the practical and emotional aspects that play a part. There are two particularly important questions that you owe it to yourself to explore as objectively as possible before determining your course:

1. Do the benefits I derive from this relationship outweigh the costs or vice versa?
2. Are my narcissistic and childlike needs and expectations pushing me toward breaking the relationship for the wrong reasons?

These questions are so crucial to your decision-making process that it will be useful to approach each one systematically.

A BENEFIT/COST ANALYSIS

No matter how good a relationship is, costs are involved—even if the cost is only the loss of some degrees of freedom that must always accompany a relationship. And no matter how bad a relationship is, there are some benefits derived. Basically, the question of whether it would be best for you to remain with or to leave your partner depends on your evaluation of whether the benefits you receive from being with him largely overbalance the costs or whether the price you pay is too high for the good things you derive. But when you are in a state of turmoil about a love relationship, your thoughts and feelings are likely to be confused, making it hard to evaluate clearly just what the relationship gives you, where it fails you, and where it may harm you. It would be nice if there was a balance sheet on which you could add up the pluses and minuses and come to an answer as definitive as the bottom line in an accountant's ledger, but that's not possible in the complex area of human emotions. So while the following self-evaluation inventory of your relationship satisfactions is not designed to give you a quantifiable answer as to what actions you should take, it can help you to think more clearly about the relationship and to locate where you are satisfied and where you are not. It is designed to help you to make a more objective benefit/cost analysis of the relationship. You may find it useful to check, at least mentally, what your evaluation is of the following important dimensions:

RELATIONSHIP SATISFACTIONS
VERY HIGH   HIGH   FAIR   LOW   VERY LOW
1. General emotional contentment
2. Communication
3. Companionship
4. Sharing of interests
5. Practical support
6. Emotional support
7. Growth support
8. Feeling loved by my partner
9. Feeling love toward my partner
10. Feeling respected by my partner
11. Feeling respect for my partner
12. Feeling trusted by my partner
13. Feeling trusting of my partner
14. Feeling nurtured by my partner
15. Feeling nurturing toward my partner
16. Enjoyment
17. Warmth
18. Sexual satisfaction
19. Feeling of self-esteem in the relationship
20. Desire to spend time with my partner

When you have done these ratings, look them over. Have you been fully honest? If not, make whatever changes would more accurately reflect your feelings. Then look at the areas of highest satisfaction. Are there more of them than areas of dissatisfaction? Or the reverse? The *number* of areas of satisfaction or dissatisfaction may not be as important as how important a given area is to you. For example, let us assume that the sexual area is *not* of great importance to you; then the fact that you rate your sexual satisfaction low may give it little weight on the "cost" side against other satisfactions you derive, or the fact that you rate your sexual satisfaction with your partner as high may be insignificant when weighed against dissatisfactions in areas that you consider more crucial. But if sexual satisfaction is an area you value highly, being sexually unhappy with your partner may outweigh many other positives, and being very satisfied sexually may outweigh many negatives. The weighing of these areas is unique to each person, and while only you can determine the importance of any area for your own happiness, looking at the total picture from a more objective perspective may lead you to question whether you do overvalue some areas and undervalue others, perhaps in a way that runs counter to your best interests.

To round out this overview of your satisfactions and dissatisfactions, consider whether there are some important areas not included in the Relationship Satisfactions Inventory. Ask yourself, "What do I like, enjoy, and value most about my partner? What do I dislike most? What am I most happy and pleased with in the relationship? What about it makes me most unhappy? How does this relationship help me to grow, and how does it hold me back?"

Use all this—the ratings, the subjective weighing of those ratings, your answer to these questions—to give you a sharpened sense of the satisfactions and dissatisfactions you have in the relationship. Picture these satisfactions and dissatisfactions as if they were in a balance scale, and get a feeling for which way the scale tilts. If it is clearly tilting toward dissatisfactions, then you must deal with the reasons that you are staying (Practical Considerations? Beliefs? Limerence? Attachment Hunger?). If it is clearly tilted toward satisfactions, then you must ask yourself why you want to leave (more on this last question later). To explore these questions more fully, let's look at how your benefit/cost analysis will be influenced by whether the relationship is a limerent or a nonlimerent attachment bond.

Limerent Attachment

When limerence is part of the tie to another person, it adds an enormous intensity to the Attachment Hunger. When you are "in limerence" you are pleasantly or painfully haunted by thoughts of the other person, your emotions are likely to swing between ecstasy and despair, and the longing for union with the object of your infatuation can become central to your life. Is that state of mind good or bad? Does it add to your life or detract? People who have been in the throes of such feelings differ widely in their views of these questions. One thirty-five-year-old man said:

> The pain is unbearable. . . . I haven't slept a night through in weeks, and at this moment I could say I'd give anything just to make the pain go away, just to forget about her. But I know that if you handed me a magic potion and said, 'Drink this and all the longing would be gone, all the horrible torture, all the depression and self-hate, all that sickening neediness—but neither will you again experience the delight, the feeling of excitement, the feeling of being 100 percent alive that you have when you are happily in love,' I would *not* drink the potion. I wouldn't want to live without that.

139

Others in this man's position would say just the opposite—that they would gladly give up the intense joy in order to be rid of the pain and yearning. A woman in her early forties said:

> I don't think I could ever need anyone in that old 'I can't live without you' way again. There were lots of highs, but oh, those lows! And I never felt I owned my life. Now it may be duller and less exciting; but my relationships are friendly and sane and not the center of everything. . . . What a relief!

You probably have your own opinion as to the effect of limerence. Professionals in the mental health field also debate whether it is a healthy or unhealthy state. But if you are ambivalent about remaining in a limerent but troubling relationship, the issue, as always, is: What are its costs relative to the gratifications you derive? Some examples will illustrate the complexities that go into making such a judgment.

Donna married when she was twenty-two. Three years later, while in a department store, a man asked her if she would please advise him about a gift he was buying for his wife. Everything about him excited her—the cool blueness of his eyes, the deep cleft in his chin, the clothes he wore, the way he walked, his laugh—everything. She and Mark began an affair shortly after their initial meeting, and her excitement and joy in being with him, and her constant thoughts about him when they were not together, led her to conclude that her marriage had all been a mistake. After all, she had never been so euphorically obsessed by her husband. Mark became the central—almost the only—interest in her life. They would get together erratically, on a schedule entirely of his making. He was very loving, very attentive, and very passionate when they were together, but he told her clearly and straightforwardly that he had no intention of leaving his wife and son now or in the future. She also found that he preferred her to keep things light, that he was never there when she was sick or needy, and that if she seemed depressed or upset about the status of their relationship, he would, to her terror, gallantly offer to end it. Despite the clear limitations of the relationship, Donna would focus on small things, such as his calling her when he was away on a business trip, to fan her hopes of a more complete relationship.

Donna's life narrowed down to her preoccupation with Mark. Her marriage was all but dead, her friends were weary of hearing about her travails with Mark and began to avoid her, her career suffered, and she was always feeling exhausted and sick with one ailment or another. Yet, in all her misery, in all her rational acknowledgment of the hopelessness of her position, she still felt as drawn to and excited by the blue eyes, the cleft in his chin, the way he walked, his laugh, his body, and the way he made love to her. She was convinced that no other man in the world could make her feel this way. So she clung to this relationship even though it was devouring every other part of her life. Clearly, the cost of this limerence-based attachment was, by any standards, too high. Even Donna agreed with that. She wished she could develop the strength and courage to break it.

On the other hand, there was Carole's relationship with Jack. "The slope of his shoulders and the curve of his back can occupy my fantasies and draw my feelings to him like a magnet. There is a vulnerability to it, and a sensitivity in his face, that comes to my mind whenever I think of leaving him." The frustrations that often made Carole consider leaving Jack had to do with his often being so self-involved that he would become withdrawn and have no room for her, that he would become emotionally detached and disappear from her life for long periods of time. On a few occasions, Carole did briefly separate from him, but when she weighed what she was getting from Jack against the price she was paying, she decided that the relationship, on the whole, was worth the emotional cost.

> I can't stand it when he crawls into a shell, but I'm not so much of a masochist that I would stay in it if I wasn't getting a lot. For one thing, I'm crazy in love with him, and it's wonderful to feel that way about someone. But even that wouldn't be enough to keep me in it. The main thing is that most of the times that I really need him he's there, and he's kind and empathic. So, instead of leaving him, I'm trying to find ways not to suffer when he has fits of withdrawal and to simply go about my business till he comes out of them.

Here, then, are two women, both limerently drawn to their men, both unhappy about some aspects of the relationship, yet each reaching a different conclusion. Donna knew that the cost of her relationship with Mark was too high relative to the gratifications she derived, though in fact it took several years of suffering before she could leave him. Carole also experienced pain in her limerent attachment to Jack, but she decided that, in total, it was a valuable relationship, and she decided to maintain it. Only you can decide, if you are limerently tied to another, whether what you are deriving is worth the emotional and practical cost. Since limerence can be blinding, it can be helpful to get the viewpoint of friends who are able to see the total picture. Besides making your balance sheet, with the positives and pleasures on one side and the negative effects on your emotions and your life on the other, you should also consider these questions as honestly as possible:

> What does this relationship give me that *feels* so good? Why is that so valuable to me?

> What effect does the relationship have on my self-confidence? On my day-to-day happiness?

Does this relationship tend to make me feel depressed? Worried? Tense? Does it affect my health? My sleep?

Does this relationship enhance or detract from my ability to work effectively? To concentrate? To be effective?

Does it make my life and my outlook wider, or does it narrow it down? Does it interfere in my relationships with my friends? With my developing new friendships? With my pursuing my interests and goals?

Even if the balance sheet indicates a tremendously high cost for the emotional benefits the limerent feelings give you, you may still find it hard to decide whether you should give up the relationship, try to improve it, or hang in there the way it is. But even if you decided to end it, it can be extremely difficult to go against the limerent feelings. So it is important to recognize that although limerence can be one of life's great emotional delights, there are some considerable hazards:

1. To the extent that limerence makes you idealize the other person and blinds you to his faults, it can make you feel unworthy relative to him, and you may be tempted, therefore, to settle for crumbs and great unhappiness within the relationship.

2. Your fear of chasing away this marvelous person may lead you to avoid the kind of confronting and engaging that is usually necessary to the development of a mutual and truly satisfying relationship.

3. You may tend to forget, if you ever knew, that in the making and sustaining of a good and fulfilling relationship, *limerence is not nearly enough*.

Nonlimerent Attachment

Lillian and Andrew had been "going together" for seven years. What this meant was that they spent their weekends and at least one night during the week in his apartment or hers, and that neither was dating anyone else. "I'm very fond of Andy, and he's fond of me. It's comfortable for both of us. . . . I can't say I ever felt great passion toward Andy or found myself longing to touch him or thinking about going to bed with him, but I definitely miss him if something comes up and we can't be together. . . ." Lillian was struggling with the question of ending her relationship with Andy. "I want us to be married. I want to live with him and make a life with him. And I want children, or at least one child. I don't have many years left to have children, and I've spent seven of them with Andy, who keeps telling me he likes everything just the way it is and can't see marriage and children fitting into his life. . . ."

Lillian's wish for marriage and children was real enough, though she admitted to some small ambivalence. And it was clear, in many discussions and arguments with Andy, that he was firm in his position. For six of the seven years with Andy she had been seriously thinking of leaving him. She would make this decision and unmake it, tell him it's over and then call him, go away on a vacation without him and return to him. Despite her frustration at their basic differences, and despite her absence of limerence, Lillian was as hooked on Andy as any crazy-in-love limerence-lorn romantic.

When Lillian would give reasons why she remained in the relationship, they would be statements like:

Andy has become like family. I look forward to speaking to him every night about all those little details of my day that nobody else would be interested in.

We know each other so well. Often he knows just how I feel and what I want without my asking.

144

He's there. With all the changes that have gone on in my life in the last seven years, he's the one constant.

He accepts me the way I am. How do I know someone else will?

Sometimes I long really to be in love. But I know I used to fall in love with men who didn't love me, and it was hell.

There's no guarantee I can find someone I'd want to marry and have a child with. I don't have that many child-bearing years left.

I'm terrified of dating again. It's been so long. And I hate that single scene. . . . I fantasize about sex with other men, but the actuality scares me. I become aware of feelings of hating my body and being ashamed of it.

I couldn't stand being all alone again, with no one to care about what happens to me. And maybe nobody will.

If I'm in the same position with Andy five years from now and I've blown the chance of having a child, I'll hate myself. But what if I leave him and in five years I have no husband, no child, and no Andy?

What are the emotional rewards that Lillian gets from this deep nonlimerent attachment to Andy? There is familiarity, continuity, caring, sharing, and being comfortable. These are no small benefits. And the cost? There is the absence of limerent excitement (which does not seem too important to Lillian) and the nonfulfillment of her wishes for marriage and motherhood (which she says is very important to her). Who but Lillian can evaluate her own Belief system as to the value and significance of marriage for her? Who can balance the benefits and costs of remaining with Andy or leaving him? Only Lillian can weigh accurately these intangible emotional factors.

But it will be helpful to Lillian in making the best decision if her thoughts and feelings were free both from the pressures of an unexamined Belief system (a woman must be married, must have a child to be fulfilled) and from the distortions that Attachment Hunger brings with it. There is a very real possibility that she may find no one else to marry and have a child with, particularly with her reproductive clock running out of time. And she will probably meet some rejection, and she may well be alone a lot. But there is nothing about Lillian's appearance or personality that is so unappealing as to make it likely that she'll *always* get rejected or will be alone *forever*. There is no good reason for her to believe that Andy is the only person in this world who can accept her the way she is, who could want to be with her, who would want to know the everyday happenings of her life, or who could care about her. These notions, and the terrible insecurity, shame, and anxiety that accompany them, arise largely from the Attachment Hunger level and can interfere with Lillian's making the most constructive decision she can make.

For Lillian, balancing the benefits and costs of remaining with Andy was particularly difficult because she was getting many good things from the relationship, and she liked and enjoyed Andy. But I know people who have strong nonlimerent attachments to partners from whom they get very little, partners who mistreat them, partners whom they do not like or do not enjoy. At times you see this most strikingly in old people who have been together for many years and live in impacted hatred, bickering over everything, criticizing everything, unremittingly bitter. Yet the years of familiarity, of habit and of shared history, the increased security needs and fear of being alone that often accompanies aging, and a long-standing sense of commitment often keep them from ever seriously entertaining the notion of leaving the other. But you can see the same paralysis in younger people, who in reality can be quite self-sustaining, quite mobile, and who have ample time ahead of them to build new relationships and create a new life. It is as if the Attachment Hunger needs for fusion and for security have taken over. Their survival, identity, completeness and self-esteem become bound up in maintaining this nonlimerent connection. And this is often reinforced by Beliefs on both the personal level (I am ugly, I am undesirable, etc.) and the societal level (one should always be in a close relationship, every relationship can be improved, a bird in the hand is worth two in the bush, ending a relationship is weakness, being without a relationship is being a loser, one should never hurt another person's feelings, etc.).

As with people who are hooked by limerence, if you are caught in a nonlimerent bind, you will also have to make a benefit/cost analysis if you are to determine whether what you are getting from this relationship is worth the price. And you will have to be ruthlessly honest with yourself. You will have to be honest about what you're getting and not getting from the relationship in all its aspects: emotionally, materially, sexually. It would be helpful to face such questions as: What are its gratifications? Do I get caring? Support? Sharing? Fun? Does it help me to grow and to feel good about myself? Or does it limit me and make me feel bad about myself? Is it frustrating? Depressing? Painful? And then, after the balance sheet, when you are considering the losses and the risks you will face should you decide to end it, keep in mind that it is often the nature of nonlimerent attachment bonds to make you underestimate your capacity to deal successfully with your life. Since Attachment Hunger is an infancy-spawned state, you may misperceive reality in the direction of feeling like an inadequate infant in a world too difficult for you to handle without a particular person. And that can cause you to distort the benefit/cost balance of the relationship and keep you from severing a destructive tie.

SELF-CENTEREDNESS EVALUATION

A benefit/cost analysis of something as complex and human as a love relationship can only serve as a guideline, as a structure to help you to examine the relationship and the varying degrees and levels of gratification and dissatisfaction. To complicate the decision-making process further, even if such an analysis shows a strong weighting toward unhappiness, it does not necessarily mean that ending it would be the best thing to do. You will also have to determine if that unhappiness is the result of the relationship failing to meet your *legitimate* expectations of a love relationship or if your own threshold for the *ordinary frustrations* of a close interaction is too low. And you will have to question whether your expectations that the other person always meets your needs is too high, or your tendency to end something when it becomes difficult or inconvenient is too great. This is not an easy determination to make, not only because it involves honest self-appraisal, but because of the climate of our times.

We are living in what has been called an age of narcissism. In reaction to generations of stifling subordination of personal inclinations to prescribed structures, such as marital and family role expectations, there has been a storm of righteous self-affirmation. Much of it has been a healthy counterpoint to the old and often unthinking and destructive constrictions. It has allowed us to know greater freedom and enabled us to see a wider horizon.

But it has also created its own problems. The meaning of self-actualization,* a valuable concept

* A. Maslow, *The Farther Reaches of Human Nature* (N.Y.: Viking, 1971).

148

that calls on us to pursue the fulfillment of our capacities to be creative, aware, and loving people, has often been perverted into narrow, egocentric selfishness. It has been distorted by man to mean what Althea Horner has called the *cult of self*. "Their maxim, 'if it feels good, do it,' suggests a rejection of legitimate issues of conscience and concern for others. Human values that have to do with what is moral or ethical or even simply decent are considered irrelevant and representative of early repressive forces in an individual's life. . . . Indeed, 'doing one's thing,' another maxim of those who preach and practice the cult of self, often implies that the other person doesn't count. No book title expresses this and other tenets of the cult of self more succinctly than *Looking Out For Number One*."*

In this narcissistic era, much license is given to end with impunity, even with congratulations, a close and important commitment as soon as it stops "feeling good." This increased social acceptance has been a very liberating development for those caught in truly destructive attachments. For while we have seen that we often are ruled and controlled by powerful feelings from the Attachment Hunger level, it is important to note that there is another aspect to those infant feelings besides the simple desire to attach and cling. The infant wants to attach himself to the *perfect* mothering person who *makes him feel good all the time,* and he gets angry when that person is not perfect and does not perfectly meet his needs. Today's increased social acceptance of the breaking of relationships can give that little child within us permission to come out, make demands, dominate, and, like a cranky tot, smash a toy or relationship that momentarily displeases us.

Dane provides a good example of this. He had been married to Lois for eleven of his thirty-four

---

* Althea Horner, *Being and Loving* (N.Y.: Schocken, 1978), p. 27.

years, and they had three children. The plastic container business he had started with a college friend had done very well, and he lived comfortably with his family in a stately suburban home. In the last few years of his marriage he had increasingly begun to snipe at Lois, to complain and criticize—she didn't keep the kids from being all over him when he was home, she didn't keep them quiet enough, she looked harried and a bit faded in the evening. He never told Lois, but the stretch marks from her pregnancies and the scar from a Caesarean had become almost all he could see when he looked at her body. In the early years of their marriage, the differences in some of their interests didn't bother him, but now they made him despise her. He loved to be active—to ski, ride horses, scuba, and disco. Lois was more sedentary, liking theaters, museums, dinner parties with friends, and, above all, relaxed times at home with the kids and Dane. They used to deal with these differences by each frequently going along with the other and at other times separately pursuing their preferences. But now Lois's requests that they spend time doing the quiet things together irritated Dane almost to the point of rage. And, in one never-to-be-forgotten incident, her slowness at mastering a skiing maneuver triggered such abuse and ridicule from him that Lois took off her skis and refused to ever go with him again. Dane was aware that much of the time he was going around hating Lois.

Then Dane met Sandy on a ski weekend, and she seemed to personify everything Lois was not, everything he now wanted. Sandy had never had children, and her body was unstretched, unmarked. She never wanted children and didn't understand people who did. She prized her freedom. She worked for a major cosmetics company and always looked freshly put together. And she loved outdoor activities. Dane had a very spirited horse that was hard to handle. After one day of riding together he said with excitement, "She's the only person besides me who can ride my horse." Within three months after meeting Sandy, Dane left Lois.

There are many ways we can look at this marital rupture. We can view it as the growing apart of two people with differing interests and needs, a sad but frequent-enough occurrence. We can see it as Dane's acting out a developmental crisis of his mid-thirties: Having succeeded at business and at establishing a family and home, he began to feel restless and to question where his life was heading and what he wanted now. We can see it as a function of Lois's being too immersed in her job as mother to do justice to her role as mate. And we can ask, if all this is true, why not separate? If they are now at different places in life with different needs and interests, why stay together? Particularly if we look at it from Dane's perspective, what's in it for him to remain in a marriage with a woman with whom he now feels he has little in common, who no longer excites him, whom he often hates?

Perhaps there can never be enough in it for him to make it worthwhile to continue the relationship, *but there may be*. First, there is the obvious value in keeping a family intact, particularly when the children are young. In itself, this is not enough reason for him to remain. We all know too many examples of couples who remained together "for the sake of the children" and have seen how the impacted hatred between them created a more destructive environment for those children than any separation could do. But Dane's relationship to the children he helped create and whom he presumably loves may form part of a complex network of reasons that could make it very valuable for him to stay. This complex network of reasons centers on *the possibility that by precipitously leaving he will lose an opportunity to develop into a fuller, richer, more mature person*. To the extent that he is acting on the basis of the needs and demands of the

151

little child or infant inside him, he is avoiding that growth possibility. That child in Dane and in all of us wants just one little thing, the one little thing all children want, *his own way*. That Attachment Hunger level part of Dane wants *exactly* what he wants, and if what he gets does not live up to the image of *perfectly* fulfilling his needs, then it's no good at all. If the other person does *perfectly* fit this image, as Sandy now seems to for Dane, then he loves her. If the other person does not *perfectly* fit this image, as Lois no longer does, then he hates her. (When Mommy perfectly fulfills the little child's needs, the child loves her. When she does not, he hates her.) And the image Dane may require in his partner may be his mirror image. When he says admiringly of Sandy, "She's the only one who can ride my horse," he is in part saying, "She is like me, and since I'm entranced with myself, I'm entranced with her." And, conversely, "Since Lois is not like me, she is no good, and I don't love her."

For Dane to override his impulse to end his marriage he would first have to recognize that there is a little boy within him and that part of his intense dislike of Lois and his impulse to break the relationship and be with Sandy stems from that little boy. But Dane either could not tolerate that painful recognition or did not have the patience that such self-awareness necessitates. Daring to confront one's deepest feelings entails the kind of emotional risks that Dane, who is able to take great physical risks on the ski slopes or on horseback, could not get himself to take. It takes very hard work to look at one's own motives and to struggle through the rough spots in the development of a relationship, and although Dane could work very hard in his business, the child in him had no tolerance for the type of work that involved exploring his own motives or with the give and take of maintaining and developing his relationship with Lois.

As the egocentrically ambitious Ralph Newsome

in Joseph Heller's *Good as Gold* says, " . . . I couldn't see much point in tying myself down to a middle-aged woman with four children, even though the woman was my wife and the children were my own. Can you?"*

So Dane ended the marriage and avoided this opportunity to become a less self-centered, truly "bigger" person. He lost this chance to stretch himself beyond his narcissistic boundaries to reach a point where he could take as much pleasure in caring for Lois and his children as separate and imperfect individuals as in having his own way. He chose, instead, what was for him the easy way, and in so doing sacrificed not only this growth opportunity but the many good things he had in his relationship with Lois. He surrendered the incomparable pleasure of being involved in the day-to-day development of his children. He only dimly grasped these losses because the inner child in Dane (or anyone) is oriented toward immediate pleasures. He knew only that his relationship with Lois didn't feel good and that he found something that for the moment felt better, so he wanted out. One may wonder how long Sandy would last in his life if she had a fall from the horse, broke her hip, walked with a limp, and could no longer ride or ski.

A close relationship, whether in marriage or otherwise, then, is not something that should be ended capriciously, and is never ended without some real losses. But sometimes, not only because of the frustration of your residual child needs but out of mature self-respect, it is necessary to say, "Enough. I do not wish to continue in this relationship." How can you know whether you are motivated by reasons stemming from your legitimate adult needs or by insistent complaints of the child in you that is seeking the *perfect* Attachment?

* Joseph Heller, *Good as Gold* (N.Y.: Simon & Schuster, 1979), p. 51.

Often it is hard to know. Sometimes the needs from the Attachment Hunger level and your mature needs are very similar. Sometimes your adult needs may mask and rationalize the underlying promptings from the attachment-seeking child. Sometimes the reverse may be true, as when you might self-deprecatingly label your appropriate adult expectations of the other person as childish. But with an honest and painstaking attempt at self-awareness you can discern whether it is your mature self or the Attachment Hungry infant inside you that is leading you to consider breaking a close relationship. And to aid you in this self-searching, here is a list of the kind of needs and demands the residual infant in almost anyone makes from a love relationship:

The other person must be exactly what you want him to be in general and at a given moment. If he (she) is not, you are disappointed, angry, and dismissing.

The other person must meet all your needs, including always being there for you when you want him there and not being there when you don't want him there.

The other person must make no demands and have no weaknesses or problems that create inconveniences for you, that disfigure the image of his (her) perfection, or that interfere with the gratification of your needs.

The other person must reflect glory on you, must make you look good, must have a high "trophy value."

The other person must be your psychological clone. He must like what you like, hold similar opinions, and want to do what you want to do.

The other person must anticipate your wishes and know what you want *without your having to ask*. You often find yourself saying, "If you really loved me, you would _____."

The other person must have no enduring or strong involvement with any activities, career, interests, responsibilities, or persons that interfere with his attentions to you.

The other person must not change or grow in ways that keep him from meeting your needs, following your script or upsetting your sense of security.

The other person must not change physically in ways that no longer meet the image that you found attractive when you chose the relationship. He (she) must not look older, must not show the scars of living, must not slow down and must not change shape.

If you change, the other person must instantly change to accommodate your new needs.

You are right, and all the problems in the relationship are the other person's fault.

You think of the relationship primarily in terms of what you are getting and not getting, and rarely, if ever, in terms of what you are giving or failing to give.

If the other person doesn't fulfill your expectations, he is to be disliked and even hated. You should be very critical, complain a lot, and ridicule whatever you see as his faults, idiosyncrasies, and inadequacies.

If he still doesn't shape up, who needs him?

One shouldn't have to work on a love relationship—if it's there, it's there; if it's not, end it.

These statements give you a pretty good picture of what the Attachment Hungry child is likely to want from a relationship. And that early part of you is bound to play some part in any close relationship. The question is whether that attachment-seeking infant is the loudest voice clamoring for you to break it up.

YOUR MATURE NEEDS IN A RELATIONSHIP

Let's contrast the above child needs with what the mature adult part of you would like in a close relationship. But first, what exactly do I mean when I refer to the *mature adult* part of you? It is that part of you that knows you are able to stand freely and able to sustain yourself effectively in the world. It is the part of you that knows that you exist as a separate, unique entity who has a considerable capacity to shape your life and whose worth does not depend on any particular other person. Defined that way, the mature you sounds pretty self-sufficient, even self-contained. What, then, would the mature adult part of you need or want from a close relationship? The answer is, a great deal. It would have to be a great deal for you to be willing to surrender so much freedom and to take on so many inconvenient obligations.

The mature adult wants the chance to grow, to develop new aspects of himself, to discover new strengths and to achieve a greater feeling of happiness through his close involvement with another person. And part of that growth and development is the expansion of his capacity to care for someone else, so that the other person's growth and well-being become as important to him as his own. If he achieves this, he becomes a larger person living in a larger world. The mature adult wants to increase his ability to know another person truly, to respect him, to accept who he is, both his strengths and his weaknesses. He knows he will never like everything about the other person, nor will the other person like everything about him, but he is confident that there is sufficient caring to have a reasonably good chance of sustaining the relationship. And he wants a companion, someone he can trust, someone with whom he can share his feelings, thoughts, and aspirations, someone whose goals may be different but not opposed to his, someone he can lean on when there is need, and someone who he is

156

willing to have lean on him. But he does not want or need a relationship based on this leaning but on the encouragement of each of the fullest development of the other's individuality. In fact, he has confidence that should the relationship not work out or should it end for any reason, and no matter how painful its ending may be, his worth, his ability to stand up and to value and enjoy his life will not be destroyed.

This is an idealized picture, but these mature needs exist in varying degrees in everyone, though their strength in comparison to each person's Attachment Hunger may differ widely. And just as this mature part of you has many specific requirements in an important relationship, it can have corresponding reasons to end such a relationship.

Suppose, for example, the Attachment Hunger level in your partner is so dominant that it leads him to demand a relationship with you in which he expects you to center your whole life around him and to live primarily to serve his need for attention and security. Your partner's controllingness can then be so great and so limiting to your own development that unless you can find some satisfactory way to deal with it, you may have to end the relationship to avoid strangulation.

Or suppose your partner is so upset at your being a separate person or at your growth that he repeatedly becomes ill or falls apart in an unending attempt to keep you chained down.

Suppose that he or she becomes abusive, either physically or emotionally, and treats you with frequent cruelty, disdain, and lack of basic respect.

Suppose he is incapable of reciprocity—the emotional give and take a relationship requires—and wants you to meet all his wishes, although he makes few if any attempts to know, understand, and meet your legitimate needs.

Suppose you found that his fear of closeness was so great that he defended against it by closing off, by coldness, by keeping you at such a distance that all your own needs for intimacy and sharing were being denied.

Suppose these kinds of frustrations and deprivations have become so chronic and pervasive that much of the joy and love have been drained out of the relationship.

And suppose your best efforts to work out and improve the relationship were unsuccessful.

In such situations, it would be the mature adult part of you that might conclude that there is little or nothing in the relationship that adds to your well-being and much that is destructive to it, and that the best thing you could do would be to end it.

How could you be sure that this conclusion was based on mature thinking and not a reaction of that part of your Attachment Hungry infant that wants a perfect meeting of his needs?

First, the mere fact that you would be attempting to discern whether it is the mature part of you or that demanding child part of you that wants to break the relationship indicates that more adult considerations are at least partly involved.

The more mature part of you would be willing to confront your own perceptions and motives and to work on your own contribution to the conflict.

You would try to stop your end of a destructive interaction, thus making it difficult for the other person to continue repeating the pattern alone.

You would be willing to face the issues with the other person and work on them as part of a joint problem.

You would be willing to give that work time, to give the other person time, and to give yourself time to more thoroughly understand yourself and each other, and to see if there can be gratifying changes in the interaction. (Remember that in Attachment Hunger you are on Infant Time—this moment is all there is, and you must end any frustration *now*.)

If you felt it might be useful to go into psychotherapy or counseling by yourself or with the other person, you would do so.

And, finally, the mature adult part of you would understand that the other person could not possibly meet all your needs or fulfill all your expectations, and you would seek other constructive ways of fulfilling your needs rather than immediately concluding the relationship is no good and prematurely giving up on it.

These, then, are some of the guidelines you might use in determining whether your *motives* for wanting to break a relationship have their origin more in your attachment-seeking inner child's demand for perfect and untaxing gratification or in your legitimate adult needs. Combined with your analysis of the benefits and the emotional costs of the relationship, you have a useful framework for exploring whether it is in ending or maintaining that relationship that you best do justice to yourself.

III

BREAKING
THE ADDICTION

13

BREAKING AN ADDICTIVE MARRIAGE

At about 3 A.M. on many of those nights when sleep eluded her, Dorothy would let herself know, with chilling clarity, that she no longer loved Ted and that she was chronically and irreparably unhappy in her marriage. But when she imagined what it would be like if she were to end it, anxiety would send her stumbling to the bathroom in panic to gulp some Valium. This had been going on for over five years, during which she had spent countless sleepless nights and consumed a lot of Valium, but she made no serious moves to put an end to her marriage.

She had long given up on the possibility of being happy with Ted. Not that she saw him as an awful person—clearly he worked hard, was a good provider, and took his responsibilities seriously—but as far as emotional responsiveness, it was as if his clock was stuck at noon and he was perpetually out to lunch. He would look uncomfortable when she spoke to him about something involving her feelings or her needs and would retreat into his endless paper work of lists, accounts, plans, etc. There were times when she would be tense or feel overwhelmed, and she would beg, "Just put your arms around me, just hold me for a minute," and he would look at her helplessly and turn his back. His sexual interest had waned to the point that they made love once every month or two, and it was usually quick and unfeeling. She had gone through stages of talking to him, seducing him, pleasing him, explaining her needs, and screaming at him, and each effort would produce some momentary change, but then he would become as removed as ever. She had insisted, a few years before, that they go for therapy as a couple. He went with her for two sessions, and then told the therapist, "That's just the way I am," and refused to go back despite the therapist clearly advising him that the marriage was in great peril.

Soon after this aborted therapy experience, Dorothy, going against strongly entrenched values, began to have an affair with a married man whom she had met where she worked as a part-time receptionist. She was driven by unsatisfied yearnings for closeness, for sex, for fun, for feeling wanted, and for being valued. And she also hoped that if she could satisfy these needs elsewhere, it would enable her to remain in her marriage. But the sweet concern, the tenderness, the laughter, and the sexuality of her lover served only to highlight how cheated she felt in her marriage to Ted. Though she felt repelled by Ted's nightly presence at her side in bed, she could not think seriously about leaving him without so much anxiety that she would dismiss the idea and brace herself for another day.

With all the deprivation she felt, what were the counterbalances within Dorothy to her wish to end her marriage? We will see that feelings from the Attachment Hunger level, as in any interpersonal addiction, are powerful and run deep. But more than any other type of relationship, the motivations arising from the levels of Practical Considerations and Beliefs (see chapter 2) play an enormous and often crucial role in the decision to terminate or maintain an unfulfilling marriage. And this is particularly true when there are young children involved. Let's look at how these levels work in Dorothy's situation in particular and how they influence such decision making in marriage in general.

Practical Considerations

Lying wide awake in her bed in the early morning hours, Dorothy would ponder the impact of a divorce on her two children, Jennifer, twelve, and Edward, nine. She knew all the clichés about how a bad marriage could be worse for children than a broken marriage, but was that really true in her case? Ted was not a bad father. It's true he seemed to have no more personal communion with the kids than he did with her, but he took his responsibilities to them seriously, chauffeuring them to activities on weekends, teaching them tennis, helping with the homework, and lecturing them, perhaps too lengthily, when they misbehaved. That was a lot more than what many other fathers she knew did, and the children, though frustrated by his distance, seemed to love and respect him. How could she deprive them of his presence? And how could she deprive Ted of the precious daily contact with them? It's not as if the marriage was bad in a way that was traumatic or destructive to the children — then she could perhaps clearly say that ending it would be the best thing for them as well as for her. But for Jennifer and Edward it would be as if their world collapsed, and for Ted it would be a painful and bewildering disaster.

And there were also the economic considerations. Ted made a good income as a vice-president of an accounting firm, good enough so that they had a comfortable suburban home, two cars, and many amenities and luxuries. But she knew that there would be marked changes in their living standard if Ted's income had to support two homes and different life goals. Could the children still go to camp? How differently would she have to shop? Was it practical to keep the house? Could she get a better-paying job? Would she need to go back to school to train for a career?

There was also the matter of the place that she and Ted, as a couple, had in the community. Ted was on several church and civic committees, she was on the school board, but even more importantly, a social life as a couple among couples was the center of their leisure-time existence. Much of that would end, to be replaced by what? All those roots, rudely ripped up. Would what was left be viable?

Such Practical Considerations are far more important in breaking up a marriage than in unmarried love relationships. The longer the marriage, the more complex the ties and the more varied the roles—husband, wife, provider, homemaker, father, mother, host, hostess, community participant, administrator, fixer, etc.—the more difficult it is to sever the relationship. To end it is not merely to cut a connection to one person, which can be difficult enough, but to a whole way of life. No parent ends a marriage without considerable concern for his children, for his relationship with his children, and, often, for the children's relationship with the other parent. A mother considering ending a marriage may have these kinds of concerns:

I'll most probably get custody of the children, but what if I don't? What if my husband fights me for custody? What will that do to the kids?

Do I really want custody? Can I handle the children mostly alone? Can I discipline them and take care of their needs on my own? And will that leave me any time and energy for myself?

Is it fair to turn the children's world upside down just because I'm unhappy? Wouldn't it be better to wait till they are grown?

Will they hate me for what I've done? For breaking up their home? For hurting their father? For depriving them of his consistent presence?

I'm also turning my husband's life over, so is it fair for me also to take away from him the pleasures of being closely involved with the children's daily development?

How will the change in family finances affect my children's lives? My life? My husband's life? Will he continue to support us? What if he disappears?

Can we really survive financially if the marriage is ended?

What will happen to the friendships we had as a couple? To the activities we pursued as a couple?

A husband contemplating ending a marriage will have many similar concerns:

How will it affect the kids? Will they hate me? Can she handle it all? What will it be like to be a "weekend father"?

Should I go for custody? Would the kids want that? Could I handle it? Do I have any chance of getting it? And how can I take the kids away from her when I've already disrupted her life?

The kids will be with her all the time. What if she turns them against me?

How can I support two households? Can I take care of their needs and still have enough left for a life for myself?

167

I've put down roots here. I am somebody in this community. Now I'll probably have to live in some furnished studio where I don't know anyone. (One man remarked on the bitter irony that on the first day he went back to his home to see the children after separating, there was a letter waiting for him asking him to run for Town Council.)

In deciding whether to end a marriage, the level of Practical Considerations must be met in practical terms. The disruptions in everyone's life will be real. If you have children, they *will* be upset, possibly scarred, and it will take sensitive weighing to balance out those hurts against the damage done by their continued living in a situation in which at least one of the parents is unhappy enough to want to get out. You will have to take into account many factors: their age, the overall atmosphere in the home, the relationship you and the other parent each have with them, and the possible arrangements that can be made. Some of the concerns—the worry of the custodial parent of having the entire burden, the worry of the other parent of losing intimate touch with the children, the worry of the initiator of the separation that he will be blamed and hated by the children—can be allayed by working out a flexible custody arrangement. Of course, this presumes some amount of good will, rationality, and overriding concern for the children on the part of each parent. So you will have to question whether you believe that you and your spouse will be able to make arrangements based on the best interests of the children. For each person, the answer to these questions will differ. But the one generalization that can be made is: Because some of the disturbing effects of the separation on the children are real, the best thing you can do is explore real ways of counter-balancing them, rather than throwing up your hands as if there are no possible solutions or just plunging ahead blindly and recklessly. Similarly, unless the family is wealthy, the reality is that there will probably be a decline in the living standard of all. So, as part of your considerations, you will have to think out as rationally as you can ways that expenses can be reduced and income increased. Taking such a pragmatic approach to these problems often clarifies that, even though there are practical difficulties and irretrievable losses, there are ways to cope with them.

Dorothy, for example, began to get enough control of her panic so she could think through her practical worries. She also began to talk to people who had gone through a family breakup to see how they were handling it. She resolved that she would make every effort to work out some form of joint custody arrangement with Ted so that there would be as little disruption in the relationship between Ted and the children as possible, and she felt it could work. She dealt with her financial worries by listing cuts in expenses she could make if she had to and by seriously considering what she might do to earn more income. She realized she had always had an interest in real estate and spoke to friends in the business about what would be involved in selling real estate. As a result, she began taking real estate courses and had an offer from a realtor she knew through her church activities to begin working for him. She could see that while there would be some very real hardships for everyone, the practical difficulties were not insurmountable. When she found that she still wasn't taking steps to end her marriage, she wondered if her great concern with the practical issues had not been largely a cover-up, a rationalization for other deeper motives for avoiding a break. It does work that way for many people. They become so concerned with the seemingly insoluble practical problems, which are so tangible and obvious to themselves and others, that they fool themselves into thinking that they stay for such reality-based reasons alone. And there are instances when the realities seem truly overwhelming. For example, a woman with several young children who is totally dependent on her husband's limited income may be desperately unhappy in her marriage but may feel trapped by these undeniable practical obstacles. Men or women married to an emotionally disturbed spouse whom they have reason to believe may commit suicide or become dangerous if they left him can feel hopelessly trapped by this awful possibility. Women who are battered by their husbands, and have every reason to leave, often fear even greater abuse, perhaps violent death, if they do leave. Men or women who are quite ill and unable to function by themselves also can feel chained by their own incapacities to a spouse they despise or fear.

There is no way to make light of these shackling realities. But I have seen people in all of these situations find some way out when their motivation was strong enough. If you feel immobilized by similar grim actualities, I cannot urge you too strongly to go for counseling, perhaps at a social or family agency, with two purposes in mind. One is to get help with these practical problems from a professional who is experienced in dealing with such seemingly insoluble difficulties. The other is to help you to determine if it is primarily these realistic difficulties that are causing your paralysis or if underlying such Practical Considerations, and perhaps concealed by them, are powerful motivations from other levels, the levels of Beliefs and Attachment Hunger.

Beliefs

When Dorothy considered leaving Ted, she found that the thought seemed to violate her whole system of Beliefs, Beliefs that she had always accepted unquestioningly. "When I said, 'till death do us part,' I looked deeply into Ted's eyes and let him know, by the intensity of my tone, that I meant it. And I did, as fully as I ever meant anything. I'm not religious, so the sacrament part is not what I was pledging, but a loving commitment to him. So how can I want something so different now? And how can I hurt Ted so?"

We see many of the Beliefs that have been an integral part of Dorothy in these statements:

Marriage is forever.

Love is forever.

Marriage is a deep and unending human commitment.

I must not hurt him by breaking that commitment, no matter what.

These Beliefs are part of her heritage. They have arisen from what she was taught by her parents and by society either directly, through the people she knew, or indirectly, through books and songs and movies. To leave Ted would represent a profound change in her Belief system.

There are many commonly held Beliefs that are in clear opposition to ending a marriage:

Marriage is a sacrament, a pledge to God.

You can always work it out if you try hard enough.

Ending a marriage is a deep personal failure and reflects a weakness.

It is better to stay in a bad marriage than to end it.

Breaking a marriage is so destructive to children that it is less harmful to them if you stay together, even with troubles, than if you destroy their home base.

You must avoid hurting your parents, and ending your marriage would hurt them terribly.

Ending marriages is a basic threat to the fabric of society and social order.

Not all Beliefs come down on the side of opposition to separation. Some, as a matter of fact, like the Beliefs held by Dane in the previous chapter, can push one to end a marriage too readily:

When a marriage no longer feels good, it's pointless and masochistic to stay in it.

A marriage is not a lifetime commitment but is good only as long as it expediently gives you what you want.

It is sad if others, like your spouse and children, get hurt by the breakup, but that's life, and they have to learn to take it.

Those are some narcissistic Beliefs about marriage, and, in a decision where your life and the lives of others can be so shaken up, where there can be much hurt, it is important for you to really challenge the childlike and self-centered core of your Beliefs. But, then, are there no Beliefs a person can hold that arise on a mature level and give some support for his wish to terminate a marriage? There are, and they also are deeply held by many people:

Marriage is not bondage, and I am not committed to remain in it at all costs.

Marriage commits me to make a painstaking and courageous effort to work out the difficulties in it, but I may not be able to successfully achieve that.

If, after long and sincere effort, the marriage is still a source of misery and works against my development as a person, I would probably be better off ending it.

It is better to end a marriage than to live in ongoing hatred, anger, fear, contempt, or depression.

In deciding to end my marriage, the hurt I may inflict on others is an important consideration, but it is not an overriding one.

If I end my marriage, I will take responsibility to protect others as much as possible from the hurt that may well come from my action.

Ending my marriage may well be best for all involved.

In dealing with your own Beliefs it will be helpful, first of all, to spell out clearly what they are and how they are influencing your decision about your marriage. And then it can be important to confront your Belief system, because it may have been implanted in you so long ago, and you may take its injunctions so for granted, that you may never have subjected it to critical examination. You may never have asked yourself:

Where does this Belief come from? From my parents? My religion? My education? My intuition?

Do I still really Believe it? Does it make sense to me now, in terms of who I am today and what I have learned about life since I acquired this Belief?

Are there no exceptions, no mitigating circumstances in the application of this Belief?

Do I want this Belief system to substitute for my judgment and accumulated knowledge?

How did Dorothy reconcile her desire to end her marriage to Ted with her long-standing Beliefs about the eternal commitment of marriage?

I not only believed it would last forever, but I wanted it to very much, and I guess I also believed that wanting it so much would assure that it would all work out. I've learned a lot of sad but true things since then. I've learned you can want something desperately and work hard for it, but it still may not work out. I've learned that love can dry up without nourishing just as surely as an unwatered plant, and Ted did not nourish this relationship, and maybe he thinks I didn't, but my love for him is as dried up as dead flowers. . . . I've learned about hate—that living with him on such a diet of emotional starvation is making me hate myself for not valuing myself enough to get out . . . and I can feel a growing hatred toward Ted. I've found myself on more than one occasion daydreaming that he'd be killed in an accident on his way back from work. Bad as it is for me, it couldn't be much better for him to be living with a wife who wants to be away from you so badly that she wants you dead. . . . I used to feel I could never hurt him by leaving him, but that was before I learned how much I could hurt him by not leaving him. . . .

There was a shift in Dorothy's Beliefs that seem not to be merely rationalizations for her wish to end her marriage to Ted but a genuine reappraisal of her Belief system in light of the experiences she had accumulated over a lifetime. More and more she was making judgments and decisions in accordance with her growing awareness of the consequences of her actions rather than with her "inherited" injunctions. As a result of this shift, Dorothy could not hold onto those earlier Beliefs that marriage was a forever commitment and that ending it was the worst thing she could do to Ted, her children, and herself. But even though she had now reconciled her intention to leave Ted with her Beliefs and had made substantial progress in preparing herself to cope with some of the difficult Practical Considerations that she could anticipate, she still made no moves to end her marriage, still spent many un-sleeping hours staring into the darkness, feeling frightened, taking Valium. It was not quite as bad as before, but something still had a hold on her. And that was the deep, underlying core of feelings from the Attachment Hunger level.

Attachment Hunger in Marriage

By and large, no adult relationship can match marriage for the formation of strong and intricately woven ties on the Attachment Hunger level. The explicit commitment to be an interdependent unit creates many bonds of mature needs such as the bene-fits of sharing experiences and responsibilities and the deep satisfactions in mutual caring, affection, and support. But it also arouses and in varying degrees fulfills many of the longings of that hidden infant in us, for unending connection, for utter security, for our existence, our identity, our self-esteem, and our hap-piness. The very habits that arise in living together in an intimate and continuous mode become part of the fabric of the attachment and often a central part of our definition of who we are. The fears of and resis-tances to breaking this connection, more profoundly rooted than our Practical Concerns or our Beliefs, can make the bitterest marital bond unbreakable.

Dorothy had found a workable way to cope with the reality issues of her children and her finances and no longer held as inviolable her earlier Beliefs about marriage, but these developments, instead of strengthening her resolve, made her anxieties worse. The more she saw that leaving Ted was really pos-sible, the more frightened and immobilized she became.

I see now that I could really do it, and it terrifies me. Who am I without Ted? What would life be with-out him? On the one hand, I want him out of my life so badly I've daydreamed about his dying, and on the other hand, the thought of his not being there feels like I'm all alone in the world. At times I almost couldn't breathe with the oppression of his being next to me in bed, but now when I think of his never being there, the bed feels so empty. Eternally empty. . . . I've had exciting fantasies of how great it would be to be a woman on my own, but when I think of the actuality, I feel more like a sad little child whose parents died. What would become of me?

These fears led Dorothy to try again with Ted, to try once more to discuss her needs and dissatisfactions, to plan for weekend holidays together. But nothing changed. She became depressed. She got very angry at him and herself. And she found that this anger gave her the courage to confront the Attachment Hunger level of her feelings.

I am letting an infant run my life! I can no longer convince myself that it's a wise, compassionate, mature considered decision to live out a commitment. It's masochism, it's cowardly, and it is childish. So I'll be scared for a while, and alone for a while, and lost for a while. I know I'll get over those feelings. . . . I know I'll have a rough time for a while, and I may never find whatever happiness I'm looking for, but it can't be worse than forever living half alive. . . . Don't worry, little Dorothy, we'll make it.

She did end her marriage with Ted and was well prepared to deal with the consequences on all three levels. And in a much shorter time than she anticipated, she was more relieved and elated than frightened. She attacked her budding real estate career with vigor and began to develop new friends and a new social life. "I never had a moment's regret, except that it took me so long. But I couldn't do it until I was ready."

Again, someone else in Dorothy's position might

arrive at a different resolution. But male or female, whether a parent or not, if you basically feel you should be out of your marriage, if you feel your dissatisfactions are not from the momentary frustrations of the self-centered infant within you, yet you still are unable to take the step of making the break, it can be helpful to begin this threefold process:

1.   Develop practical means for coping with the anticipated Practical Considerations;

2.   Challenge whether you really still believe that your long-established and unmodified Beliefs offer the best guide in your current situation; and

3.   Identify and confront the infant neediness and fearfulness of the Attachment Hunger level so that you can both overrule and comfort that frightened and demanding infant, freeing your most mature you to make the wisest and most self-respecting decision that you can.

14

BREAKING WITH A PERSON WHO IS MARRIED TO SOMEONE ELSE

The most tragic and self-defeating addiction is an addiction to someone who is tied to someone else, particularly by marriage. Yet millions of people are unhappily involved with a married person, and, despite their enormous suffering, they remain in the relationship, bound by their own emotions and hopes.

Certainly there are instances where such a relationship works out—the married person leaves his or her spouse and makes a commitment to this third person. And because it sometimes happens, it is tempting to hold onto the hope and even the feeling of certainty that it will happen for you, if you are in such a situation.

Maureen, who was chronically distraught in her long-time affair with securely married Brad, demanded of me, "Surely you must know lots of cases where people have left a marriage because they were in love with someone else and wanted to be with him or her." I answered, "Yes. But for each one I know like that I know of many others who did not leave their marriage."

Maureen became defiant and angry at me whenever I challenged her. "But you know how fulfilling and beautiful it is between Brad and me. And he says that all the passion has gone out of his marriage. It feels to me like it's only a matter of time. Why are you always so discouraging?"

"You say it's only a matter of time. But how much time are you willing to give it? It's already almost three years."

"The fact that it has lasted three years, with all the difficulties we've had to go through just to be with each other, shows that he really cares and that we have something very rare and special."

"Maureen, has he ever told you he would leave his wife?"

Maureen was silent. "In fact, hasn't he told you just the opposite—that though he loves you he will never leave her and the kids?"

Maureen began to sob softly. "Why are you doing this to me?" she wanted to know.

In working with a patient who is involved with someone who is married to someone else, the therapist must often assume the role of spoiler. He must assume this role not only because he can see that the involvement is likely to be futile, but to challenge the blatant self-deceptive maneuvers that are frequently used by someone in love with a married person. Often, the married person may feed this deception, offering snippets of hope, if not outright promises. But even where he does not, it is easy to feel: "He (she) is so happy with me and so unhappy with her (him) that it just has to work out. And I am so in love with him (her) that I will hang in there till it does."

So, if you are in a long and deep involvement with a married person, you must be alert to any attempts you may be making to delude yourself. You would be well advised *to believe him* completely when he says he will not leave his marriage, no matter how loving he is. And you would be well advised *not to believe him* if he says he will leave his marriage and will be with you if he has made no moves to change his status, no matter how loving he is. Above all, it is essential to stop yourself from reading meaning into things that really give no evidence of movement toward a change in status. Brad, for example, would at times give Maureen a spontaneous little gift—a new book by her favorite author or a blouse in her favorite color—that she would take not only as a display of his affection but as an indication that he was moving toward a commitment to her. And she would do this despite his clearly having stated, many times, the limitations of the relationship.

Why do people get involved with someone who is married? And why do they stay involved if it means wanting something they cannot have? They initially may get involved for the same reasons anyone gets involved with anyone—attraction, liking, good feelings, opportunity. But when it continues well after the handwriting is on the wall, then other factors are probably at work, and usually quite unconsciously. One factor is the same one we have seen in people who form attachments to someone who is, for any reason, unattainable: the compulsion to master the failed childhood task of winning the love and attention of someone who is not giving it to you. But often there is another specific element in this triangle situation: *the fear of having a man (or a woman) of one's own.* Why would someone have such a fear? And, if he has it, why would he not simply avoid getting involved with *anyone?*

Part of the answer to these questions is in the fact that the attempt to win someone who "belongs" to someone else recapitulates the childhood Oedipal conflict. In the early years of life there is a wish to win the primary or even exclusive affection of the parent of the opposite sex: The little boy wants his mother *all* to himself, and the little girl wants her father *all* to herself. In *Cutting Loose* I wrote:

> This means the child wants to eliminate his (her) rival, the parent of the same sex, and therefore harbors death wishes toward that parent. This secret deadly competition makes the little boy fearful of horrible retaliation by his father and the little girl fearful of horrible retaliation by her mother. Ideally, as the child sees the futility of his desires, largely by noting that the parent he wants to possess does not want the same kind of relationship with him, he gives up his Oedipal wishes for the opposite-sex parent, experiences the relief of identifying with rather than competing with the same-sex parent and is free, at a later time, to find a mate all his own.*

But sometimes it is not resolved so happily. The opposite-sex parent may have been *too unavailable,* not giving the child the opportunity to experience this prototypical loving relationship with the opposite sex. Or the opposite-sex parent may have been *too available,* even seductive, thereby stimulating the child's involvement and increasing his fear of retaliation by the other parent. Or his parent of the same sex may have been so rivalrous that he made the child afraid of his own competitive feelings. Or that same-sex parent may have been so weak a rival that he did not help his child to limit his frightening impulses. And so the child can carry these unresolved feelings and taboos into his adult life.

One way that you can carry an unresolved Oedipal situation into adulthood is by becoming involved with someone already married. This nearly duplicates your situation as a child, and you may be acting out your old wish to triumph over your same-sex par-

* Howard Halpern, *Cutting Loose* (N.Y.: Simon and Schuster, 1977), p. 145 and (N.Y.: Bantam), p. 132.

ent (in the form of your lover's spouse). But at the same time you are setting it up so that you will lose again, thus avoiding the guilt and possible retaliation such a conquest would bring. And in order to keep this old drama going, you may use a lot of those self-deceiving mental gymnastics to pump up unwarranted hopes.

If we look at Maureen's background in this regard, we see that her father was an extremely intense, nervous man, always on the run, giving her sporadic bursts of affectionate attention and then hurrying off into another preoccupation. And her mother, having become exhausted by and resigned to this same erratic behavior, assumed the position of an ineffectual but bitter sniper. Maureen recalls that as a little girl she had the thought that if her mother was more assertive and cheerful, her father would calm down, stop running, and stay around more. And she could remember feeling that if she were married to her father, she could make him content and loving.

Brad was not the first married man with whom Maureen had become emotionally entangled as an adult, but it was her deepest and most long lasting of such involvements. She had met Brad when they were stuck in an elevator together in the office building in which they both worked and went to have a drink afterward to celebrate their escape from the ordeal. He wore a wedding band, talked proudly of his children, and seemed like a well-married man from this first meeting, but they enjoyed each other's company and it was easy enough to arrange to meet for lunch. They found that they both worked in the publishing business, and that gave an extra dimension to their common interests. Before too long they were meeting for dinner and began a covert affair that was deeply pleasurable for them both, but which became increasingly frustrating for Maureen. The first time they made love he had said, "You know, I will never leave my wife, so if you can't accept that, it would be better to stop now."

It is easy to see how Maureen's unresolved Oedipal feelings entered into this situation. Here was a married man, like her father, but at the same time very different from her father. He was warm and empathic and generous in his attentions—the way she always fantasied her father would be if she were his woman. So she could try to do with Brad what she never was able to do with her father—win him all to herself. But, at the same time, she was choosing to remain in a situation where her guilt over her wish to displace her mother and her fear of succeeding at this were not likely to be aroused, because the possibility of this triumph was so remote. It was, unhappily, a perfect situation for the reliving of her earlier family drama, where she could play at being victorious but never quite make it.

As Maureen and I explored this dynamic we discovered another facet to it: By arranging to remain in a situation where she could not have a man of her own, she was arranging to be her mommy's little girl forever. While at first she had said she was not particularly close to her mother—and in truth they had little of common interest—she did see her and talk to her often. Their conversations were frequently about their unhappiness with the main man in each of their lives, and they were attached by this common bond of untriumph. If Maureen were to leave Brad and find a good, intimate, and loving relationship with a man of her own, this losers' bond between her and her mother would be broken, and Maureen might feel more anxiety and guilt than she cared to face.

Similar dynamics were evident in the relationship of a thirty-five-year-old man, Dick, with a married woman. They had been having an intense and exciting affair for two years, and Dick made it very clear that he wanted her to leave her husband and marry him. The woman, Zoe, told him, no doubt honestly, that she loved him much more than she ever loved her husband, that she thought about him all the time and looked forward to their stolen hours together. But she could not get herself to leave her marriage. It became evident from things Zoe said that the obstacles to leaving were formidable for her—her guilt, her home, her life in the community, her not wanting to disrupt the lives of her two children. And it was just as clear, though never openly stated, that her husband offered considerable luxury, while with Dick they would have to live on his adequate but hardly sumptuous salary as an assistant principal of the elementary school Zoe's child attended.

Dick railed against these obstacles, but somewhere within him he knew all along that it was a lost cause. And for Dick, too, as we explored his tenacious clinging to this role of the loser, we could see the Oedipal meaning of it in a lifelong feeling of rivalry with his competitive father, a rivalry in which Dick was no match for his father's power, position, and controlling role with both his wife and with Dick. We were also able to see that by not having a woman of his own, Dick was remaining in his old mutually protective tie to his mother.

Sometimes, the tie to Mother in these situations is more symbolic than real. I have seen people whose mother has been dead for many years remain hooked into a role of being the little child who never grows up and leaves her, and often this is played out in attaching themselves to someone with whom they can never form a committed relationship. In Attachment Hunger terms, they remain connected to the earliest object of that attachment by avoiding a new primary relationship that would have the commitment, love, and leverage to come between them and that first relationship. In this way, an addiction to a married person may permit you to maintain an unconscious and unbroken tie to the first Attachment Hunger person of your early years.

Before we go on to discuss specific steps in breaking your addiction to someone married, let's also take a look at your partner's role in keeping the frustrating relationship going, because often, if you observe it closely, you will see that a destructive game is being played. If we watch Brad, for example, we might ask, "What is he up to? On the one hand he tells Maureen he'll never leave his wife, while on the other hand he is the compleat and thoughtful lover. These are double messages that seem aimed to tie Maureen up in knots." In working with Maureen I noticed that every time she was beginning to make progress in her efforts to break off with him, two things would happen. First, she would tell me that Brad had said that as much as he loved her, he knew it was best for her to end it and make a new life for herself. Then, very soon after, she would tell me of some "sensitive note" or "thoughtful little gift" that she received from Brad that "no one else would think of." She would begin to feel, "How can I leave such a wonderful man?" and "He must love me to be so tuned in to me." Her progress toward leaving him would founder.

Appearing to be such a loving and empathic man was a game on Brad's part, whether it was conscious or not. While telling her that she can't have him, he does what he must know will be effective in holding her. He is saying, "You can't have me" but "See how marvelous I am." It is, beneath the seeming lovingness, a cruel game of "Eat your heart out." If you are caught in a bind like this, it is important that you recognize the hard truth that he or she has Attachment Hunger needs so great that he is trying to hold onto both his spouse *and* you. If he does not want to end his marriage, the most maturely loving thing he could do for you would be to completely, unconditionally, and irrevocably get out of your life. It is not love but self-indulgence that leads him to hang in there, feeding you the poisoned sweets of false hope.

How do you know if your continued involvement with someone married is based on unfounded hopes or is a realistic appraisal leading you to take a well-calculated gamble? As I indicated earlier, such relationships sometimes do work out. In fact, some of the happiest marriages I know were born out of this unhappy and distressful situation. How can you tell if you will be one of the lucky ones or not?

You can never know for sure. But you can gain a lot of clarity if you recognize the possibility of self-deceit and push yourself to look at the facts clearly. What does the person say? Do his actions concur with his words? Are you reading more into little gestures and ambiguous words than is really meant? Do the two of you talk of *detailed* (rather than romantically fuzzy) plans of a future together? Is he taking any *concrete* steps to change his status? How long has it been going on? How would you feel if it were going on exactly like this a year from now? Two years from now? Five years from now? Have you asked friends who know you and the situation how they see it, and what they think you should do? What do they tell you?

Because it is a situation with so many levels of motivations, such complex interactions, and enormously compelling tendencies to self-deception, it can be one of the most difficult love addictions to break. To help you to determine if you are, indeed, fooling yourself and to help you to end your addiction, if that is what you want to do, I suggest applying these six guidelines:

1. Unless there is hard and firm evidence that he or she is moving toward an explicit and concrete change in his commitments, stop deluding yourself that it will all work out.

2. You will also have to stop deluding yourself that you are more important to him than his spouse, his marriage, and his children. If you are, he would leave and be with you. Marriage and family can be very powerful emotional investments.

3. You will have to set a reasonable time limit

in your mind as to how long you will wait to see if he will make any changes in his status and commitments. And then, if there are no changes, you will have to adhere to that deadline or you can drift on endlessly.

4. Stop idealizing him (or her). Note that the game he may be playing with you—of giving you enough to keep you involved but not the commitment you want—is not a loving game. It means that in this regard he is not Mr. Clean, Mr. Nice Guy, Mr. Ultra Desirable, or Mr. Mature. Rather, there is a childlike selfishness at work in him in regard to both you and his spouse, and you ought to look at that squarely.

5. It can be useful to prepare your friends to be there for you when you go through the inevitable withdrawal symptoms and to help you to maintain your resolve to break it when the going gets rough. (For more detail about the uses of such an addiction-breaking network and how it was helpful to Maureen, see chapter 16.)

6. In general, and perhaps most important, deal with the probability that if you have been choosing to remain with a person who is committed to someone else, you may be avoiding having a close relationship with a man (or woman) *of your own.* An exploration of your motives, along the lines that proved helpful to Maureen and to Dick, could also be quite helpful to you.

All this may be of use both in breaking the demoralizing attachment you are now in and in making you aware of the unconscious, Attachment Hunger meaning of the relationship. This insight can help you to prevent repeating a similar futile pursuit in the future. For the truth is that you are not a child who must settle for being on the outside of a primary bond. You are entitled to the grown-up privilege of having a loving partner all your own. But you will never have that privilege unless you free yourself from the unavailable married person to whom you are addicted.

15

ADDICTION-BREAKING TECHNIQUES: THE USES OF WRITING

"Okay, I understand it. I understand that all those feelings and needs from the Attachment Hunger level are pushing me to hold onto a relationship that is no good for me. But still I can't let go. What now?"

For some people, recognizing that they are being compelled by feelings from the past to cling to a bad relationship is enough to enable them to take decisive steps to end it. But for most people, this general awareness is not enough. It may move them a bit closer by putting their dilemma into a new framework, but they still feel trapped and bewildered about how to use this new insight to sever the unwanted tie. So in this and the next two chapters we will discuss in detail some techniques you can use to break your addiction to a person. These *techniques* should not be confused with the central *tasks* to be worked on and achieved in this process. It is the difference between means and ends. There are three major tasks leading to the overall goal of leaving a relationship once you have decided that you should leave:

1. Recognizing and freeing yourself from your own particular Attachment Hunger (addictive) feelings that are preventing you from leaving the relationship.
2. Recognizing and putting a stop to the specific self-defeating mental processes that keep you immobilized.
3. Maintaining your sense of identity and self-worth without the Attachment Fetish Person.

Any techniques that can help accomplish these tasks can be useful. Many have been invented by my patients, and you, too, may want to innovate, to custom-design methods that will be particularly helpful for you. There is nothing wrong with "gimmicks" as long as they move you closer to your goal and have no significant harmful side effects. The use of specially tailored writing techniques can be particularly helpful.* Below are some writing exercises that you might find helpful in breaking your addiction.

1. A Relationship Log. Some people regularly keep diaries. Most people kept them at some time in their childhood or adolescence, perhaps with great dedication, but then their entries became more sparse and stopped. But if you are in a troubling relationship, I urge you to keep a particular type of diary—a Relationship Log. Keep track of the events and happenings of the relationship, but above all, and in as hon-

* For most of these techniques, tape-recording can do just as well. There is some advantage to writing as you can look back on it in a glance, and because writing, being a very evolved, high-level activity, can counterpose the more primitive infant level flow of feelings and thoughts that compose the Attachment Hunger. But if you hate writing, or are more an oral and auditory person, then by all means use tape.

189

est detail as you can, set down your *feelings* about the contacts with your partner. The reasons this can be extraordinarily helpful are: (a) It compels you to *notice* what is going on and how you feel about it, (b) It can help you to look back through it and see the *shape* of the relationship, what it has really been like and felt like, what has been its patterns over time, and (c) It can curb your tendencies to *distort* the relationship by either twisting events, repainting your feelings and forgetting either the unpleasant (which may get erased by our Attachment Hunger) or the pleasant (which may get erased by your anger). Jason, for example, had been in a three-year highly volatile relationship with Dee, a woman who at times was exciting, loving, and responsive, but more often was selfish and careless about his needs and feelings. Several times, overwhelmed by frustration and feelings of deprivation, Jason would stop seeing Dee, but in a matter of days or weeks he would begin to "forget" the reasons he left, or at least forget how awful these incidents made him feel. I suggested that he keep a log of the relationship, to try to write in it the events and feelings of each significant contact. He was amazed at how much more frequently he was recording bad feelings—disappointment, hurt, incredulousness about her selfishness, rejection, rage at her demandingness, frustration at trying to talk things out reasonably—than he was writing of feelings of loving, feeling loved, tenderness, happiness or serenity. And at one point when he did stop seeing Dee and was beginning to feel only the missing her and to remember only the golden times, he looked back over the previous eight months of his Relationship Log (he called it "Me & Dee") and had his fading memory rudely jogged. There were entries like this:

> What a bitch! I practically never get sick, but a virus really hit me today, fever of 102, shaking chills. Spoke to Dee in morning. She said she was too busy to come

over — was meeting a friend for lunch and shopping. She didn't even call till late that night. Sent flowers, though! Screw the flowers.

(Until Jason read that entry he had half forgotten the incident, and the half he remembered was how wonderful she was to send flowers!) Another entry:

My car hit a pothole today, and the shock absorber broke. Can't use the car till it's fixed tomorrow. Told Dee about it — that I couldn't drive her to airport, she'd have to take cab or something. She screamed about never being able to count on me, hung up on me. I can never do enough for her. I feel like dumping the bitch.

And this:

Party at Ken's place. Dee flirted with every man there. Saw her slip one guy a folded up piece of paper. Her phone number? We had fight after. She denied all, accused me of being paranoid and trying to keep her caged. But I know what I saw. Couldn't sleep.

There were many more such entries, interspersed with loving moments, one or two particularly ecstatic sexual encounters and an idyllic weekend at a beach motel. But the main emotional motif of "Me & Dee" was torment, and it was enormously helpful to Jason, even a comfort, when he read it in the grip of his withdrawal suffering.

If you have not kept a Relationship Log and are now about to end the relationship or are in turmoil because you have ended it, it is not too late to do it from memory. It will not be as accurate as one done "on the spot," and it can suffer from distortions, but it is still worth doing if you make a commitment to yourself to be as honest as possible. Use whatever aids you may have in reconstructing — photos, friends, mementos—and try to recall the feelings around a given incident. Try to give form and detail to the formless way you may now experience the relationship so you can understand exactly why you wanted to end it. Take it out and read it when the feeling of missing this person becomes so great that you might be tempted to overvalue him or to forget the unpleasant side.

2. *Finding the Patterns.* It can be eye opening to see if there is a *pattern* in the people you have tended to get involved with and the types of relationships you have formed, so unless your current partner is the only love relationship you have had, I suggest you do a Relationship Review. First, list the names of each person with whom you have had a romantic attachment, going as far back as you can. Then set down the Physical Attributes of each—his or her height, build, hair color, movement, voice, general attractiveness, etc. There may well be a pattern, because most people have preferences. *The question is whether these physical preferences have been so strong as to block you from seeing the person's other characteristics accurately.*

After noting the Physical Attributes, write down the Personality Characteristics of each person on your list. What do you feel is the most striking feature of his personality? What adjectives best describe him: Introverted or extroverted? Passive or active? Warm or cold? Intimate or distant? Self-confident or self-effacing? Successful or ineffectual? Hearty or frail? Independent or dependent? Mean or kind? Submissive or aggressive? Did your view of his personality change from the early days of the relationship till later on? If so, how soon did you really have indications that all was not what it seemed?

In chapter 8 I wrote of a woman named Jeanne who acknowledged that she had "always been drawn to men with a broken wing or some tragic flaw," but Jeanne did not always have that insight. At first she insisted that she was attracted only to dashing, handsome, self-confident men but somehow things didn't work out. When she wrote her Relationship Review, an underlying pattern clearly emerged—beneath the surface charm and glitter the men she chose were always weak, tortured, and dependent. She realized that she had the evidence for it very early in the relationship but chose to ignore it. With one man, on their first date he had recounted a history of holding many jobs for brief periods, always giving a glib explanation for why he quit or was fired, always talking of lofty ambitions that were, looked at objectively, not very realistic. With another man she could see on their first few dates that he was drinking much too much but chose to accept his explanation of a need to unwind after a tough day. Jeanne began to face the possibility that since many of these men were "broken winged" and she "knew" it right from the start, her attraction was not to the dashing man but to the loser, and this led her to discover her pattern of trying to solve the unresolvable task of her childhood—how to prop up her handsome but weak father (see page 95). So, once you have listed the Personality Characteristics of the people you have had relationships with, look it over and see what commonalities emerge and what these commonalities suggest to you.

Even more important than similarities in the physical and personality characteristics of people with whom you have had close relationships are the Relationship Characteristics, the repeated *patterns of interaction* in which you have been involved. To get some idea if your relationships have had repeated patterns, it can be useful, under the name of each person with whom you have had a relationship, to write the answers to questions such as these:

1. Exactly how did the relationship start? Who was the initiator? The pursuer?
2. Was one of you more dominant? Who seemed

to control when and where you would get together, and how you would spend your time?

3. What was the emotional tone of the relationship for you? Loving? Angry? Contented? Depressed? Anxious? Boring? Insecure? Romantic? Desperate? Or what?

4. Emotionally, did you get your needs satisfied?

5. What was the sexual aspect like? Were you happy with it? Unhappy? Delighted? Disappointed? Angry?

6. How did the relationship end? Who ended it? Why? What were the feelings of each of you about its ending?

7. In the cost/benefit analysis, was what you were getting worth the price?

By reviewing your relationship you can often uncover startling insights into patterns you may not have noticed. For example, Jason, who took so much abuse from Dee, had always seen it as an unfortunate happenstance that he fell in love with someone so selfish and ungiving. But, after reviewing his relationships, he sadly concluded:

> You know I've never been involved with a really loving woman, with a woman who took pleasure in making me feel good. They were all self-involved and mean spirited, even though some of them were great at the grand gesture, at the generous theatrical act that would seem so loving, such as giving me an unexpected present that she thought I'd like, or a surprise party, or a special sexual encounter. And I fell for those big dramatic gestures every time, even though on a day-to-day basis I was frustrated and starving. . . . Even the first girl I fell in love with, when I was nine years old, was an icy little princess. I worshiped her, and if every now and then she smiled in my direction, I would forget that she almost totally ignored me. . . . Why have I

never permitted myself a relationship that really made
me feel good?

That last question was a direct outgrowth of Jason's Relationship Review and was a turning point in
his life. He was able to see that, first of all, his relationship with Dee was not an isolated event but part
of a long-standing pattern and that, therefore, he had
to take responsibility for choosing such relationships.
This led him into a deeper trip of self-discovery. He
could see that, beginning with his mother, he had repeated again and again the futile attempt to get love
from women who had severe defects in their capacity
to love. It was a critical step in his being able to end
his demoralizing and demeaning relationship with
Dee, and to begin to move toward women who could
offer him more of what he wanted.

3. *Memos to Yourself.* A patient of mine invented
the technique of writing memos to herself (chapter 3,
page 28). She used them to keep an adult time perspective as she went through the withdrawal pains of ending her relationship with Wayne. She wrote them
from "Big Me" to "Little Me" and recorded such ad-
vice as: "You will feel terrified of the eternal pain of
eternal loneliness. But that's just your infant view of
time. As an adult I can assure you that there is a
tomorrow, and I promise you that you will feel better
again." Perhaps because she was an Administrative
Assistant, writing memos came to her more spontaneously than the log I had suggested she keep during
withdrawal, and she was able to use it in many other
ways than keeping her time perspective. She knew,
for example, that coming home to an empty apartment after work was a particularly dreadful time for
her in which she felt terribly alone and incomplete.
So she would write memos, *mail them* to herself, take
them out of her mailbox when she got home the following night, and find such things as: "Hi! Welcome

home. Make yourself that curried chicken, and put on some good music. You are worth making a fuss over. After, get to that stack of letters and bills you've been putting off." Or, "Call Carolyn and/or Mabel tonight and make some plans for the weekend. Then enjoy the rest of the evening by doing whatever you want to do that would be fun and pleasureful." Or:

> Tonight will be exactly two weeks since you last saw Wayne. If I know you, you'll get particularly sad and sentimental over the anniversary and may even be tempted to call him. You'll begin to forget why you ended it. So remember how impossibly stingy he was and berated you viciously for being extravagant whenever you bought something a little luxurious, even though it was with your own money! And how stupidly meticulous he could be. And how ungenerous he was with his feelings. It's the two-week anniversary of being free of all that.

Since then I have suggested to others writing such memos and each has elaborated on the technique, using it to deal with all phases of the ending of the relationship. Jason, who was in therapy with me at the time, wrote what he imagined I would tell him when he was suffering withdrawal pangs. Interestingly, they were not the "clever interpretations" I made that he put in his memos, but phrases like "she's no bargain" that he found particularly helpful at moments like that. What these memos all had in common was that they were ways of stimulating the writer's perspective, memory, and judgment when these faculties were threatened with being swamped by a tidal wave of Attachment Hunger needs and emotions. So I elaborated on the memo theme, seeking other ways to help people get in touch with their most mature selves when they were most in danger of drowning in residual infant turmoil. One technique was to suggest that they write memos to themselves from "the wisest sage in the world—one who saw life clearly, compassionately, and with great perspective." This sage once wrote to Eileen, "Certainly you can't believe your life is over or that you are meaningless without this one man among millions of men? Or without any man? Life is bigger than that. You are bigger than that." (For another example of this technique, see chapter 7, pp. 69 to 71.)

A variation on this, derived from Transactional Analysis, is writing memos from your idealized parent, a parent who is clear thinking, rational, loves you deeply, and is 100 percent on the side of your best interest. Eileen found this technique particularly helpful in breaking with Peter, perhaps because her real parents had not given her sufficient backing and support to have developed a sense of independent strength. Her mother was not a very empathic woman and made it clear that she was pleased with her only when she was quiet, well mannered, and reflected well on her parents. Her father, who was away much of the time with the merchant marine and was distant even when he was home, did not seem to know her at all. One time, almost two months after Eileen left Peter, she had gone to Paris on vacation with a friend, Mandy. After the first week of a planned two-week stay, she was in such an anguish of missing him that she told her friend that she would have to return home immediately. She said that she could tell from how much she missed him that she truly loved him and would go back to "where I belong—with Peter." Mandy was too angry at her to talk her out of it effectively, and Eileen went off to the airport. She got to the airport almost three hours before take-off, and, sitting there all alone in the fluorescent-lit waiting room, she began to question what she was doing. She took out some paper and began to write a memo from her idealized parent. It read in part:

> Eileen, honey, you set yourself up for this. It was just too soon after the breakup to take yourself to one of the most romantic cities in the world. How could you

expect you wouldn't feel lonely and miss him? But missing him doesn't change anything. It doesn't mean you love him, it only means you miss the feeling of being in love. Peter is still Peter, and if you go back now, it will be the same old nightmare, only worse. . . .

Eileen reported that her mood shifted as she wrote these words. "I began to feel free again, good. I canceled my airline ticket and called Mandy, telling her I was coming back to the hotel."

Whatever way you can create to use these memos to hold onto or restore your perspective, it is an effective and helpful approach. I suggested it to Arthur, a man who was remaining endlessly in a relationship with Betsy, a woman he did not love, for fear of being alone and of being rejected by other women. He invented his own variation, perhaps in keeping with his tendency to plan his life in orderly detail. He made up a series of pre-written memos, memos that he could later take out and look at as needed. They were brief and pointed, written from "the father I wish I had had":

You don't love her. You'll never marry her. If you want to be married some day, you must leave her.

Leaving her will hurt. You will survive it. Any feeling you have to the contrary is from the infant in you and has nothing to do with reality.

You are no movie star. You will get rejected by some women. So what? You will survive that, too. You are attractive *enough*. You have much to offer.

Arthur wrote dozens of such pre-composed memos. Simply writing them helped him move toward breaking with Betsy. Later, while going through the painful process of making and sustaining the break, he would look through them and hold onto his perspective. He would tack up on the bulletin board in his bedroom the ones that were most pertinent to where he was at that moment. He found it enormously helpful, and you, too, could benefit from these pre-planned memos. Here are some examples taken from several other people:

> Remember how he was cold and ungiving, even the time your father died.

> I am a definite, worthwhile and *complete* person without him.

> No matter how much you miss her, you know, when you are thinking clearly and even in your heart of hearts, that she is wrong for you.

> Just because I hurt so much doesn't mean I love him. It means I'm an addict in withdrawal.

You know yourself. You know what feelings and distortions you will be up against when you end it. So from the most rational you, write the messages you will need to read when you are suffering most.

4. Making Connections. To free yourself from the tyranny of your Attachment Hunger, it can be helpful to see clearly the connection between the infant or child you once were and the feelings you are experiencing now. Earlier (page 38) I discussed a man who discovered that the terror he felt when he thought of ending a destructive relationship had early roots. He had been talking of the fear that he was abandoned, that he would be alone forever, that no one would ever love him. I asked him to push back along his time track to try to recall earlier and earlier memories of this feeling. After a while he remembered the incident when he awoke one night in his crib, very thirsty, and cried out for his parents. They did not come for a while (it is not clear for how long) because they had dropped over to visit their next door neighbor. As I wrote before, "He could remember the feeling that they were gone forever, and he would die. He recalls that after screaming for what seemed like an eternity he curled up in a corner of the crib whimpering. And he knew that these were the same awful feelings he anticipated if he ended his current unhappy attachment." This led us to explore further, and we could see that this incident was as powerful as it was in his feelings not solely because it was in itself traumatic but that it stood for a whole atmosphere in which he felt that his parents, rather detached people, were often emotionally unavailable even when they were physically there. This led, in turn, to further exploration of incidents around their unavailability and the feelings this generated in him, feelings of fear and neediness that had become part of who he is and that could govern his life.

Seeing this connection so vividly, rather than as an abstract theory, was very useful to this man in coping with his feelings and eventually in decreasing their power over him. It would also be enormously helpful for you to connect up with the infant and child memory tapes within you. Write down each negative feeling that is triggered by anticipating or acting to break a bad relationship, whether it is your terror of aloneness and abandonment, overwhelming neediness, longing, inadequacy, insecurity, guilt, or whatever. Then, for each, think about and write down whatever you can remember of the earliest times you felt like that. What was going on? Why did you feel that way? What in the present situation seems similar enough to be triggering these old feelings? Is it really a valid and appropriate way for you to be reacting now? Feel the connections, be compassionate, empathic, and supportive to the little child you once were—he had reason to feel the way he did. But you will probably discover that you, as an adult, do not have good reason to feel now as you did then. And that can be very liberating.

16

ADDICTION-BREAKING TECHNIQUES: A SUPPORTIVE NETWORK

There is a popular song that tells us that "breaking up is hard to do." It is particularly hard to break an important relationship all by yourself. The very nature of ending a close relationship, especially when you are addicted to the other person, arouses feelings so basic, so frightening and painful, that they can paralyze your will and cause you to cling compulsively, even desperately, to the very relationship you are trying to break. There are few situations in which you are more likely to need a little help from your friends. At a time when you are breaking a connection which has given you sustenance, friends can serve as an auxiliary life-support system. For some people, one friend on whom they can count works better than a group of friends. But for most people, having a network of friends who are on their side and willing to help has some very powerful advantages. For one thing, since you are likely to feel very needy and very repetitive in talking about the situation, you may easily sense that you could wear out the welcome of even the staunchest and most well-intentioned friend if you put the full burden of your neediness on him alone. Second, you will have more eyes observing you and reflecting back what they see of you and your situation. Third, different friends will have differing things to offer. Some will always be available and some will not. Some will offer tenderness and others toughness; some you will be able to talk to about your deepest levels of feelings and motives, others will help you to keep things light and humorous; some will have objective judgment that you can trust, others will be blindly on "your side" or have their own axes to grind. All are valuable, may supplement each other, and together form a network of handholders, soft shoulders, hard confronters, directional compasses, and ego filling-stations that can provide a base for your addiction breaking.

The value of this network is so great that having it or not having it should not be left to chance. It can make the crucial difference in your success in ending the relationship. It has many specific and even specialized uses, but overriding all else is that when you are terrified of being all alone in the universe, it can give you the comforting assurance that there are other caring people out there. And this assurance, by making you feel reconnected to the web of life, can firm up your determination to make and sustain the break.

Forming such a network requires trust. If you have not been a trusting person in general, it can seem particularly difficult to trust people at a time when you are increasingly vulnerable, but you can use the urgency of the crisis in your life to motivate you to take a risk. If you do not have many or any friends to take this risk with, that fact is probably telling you much about why you became addicted in the first place—that you put too many of your needs into this one relationship for lack of other relationships. It may also be saying that your addiction to that one relationship narrowed your world so much that there are now not enough other connections. And perhaps your love relationship is an unhappy one, in part because it was overburdened with too many of your attachment needs. Before you try to take the necessary steps to break your addictive relationship, you might address yourself to developing friendships so that you don't need to fear you would be ending the only relationship that stands between you and complete isolation.

If forming friendships has been difficult for you, it is not likely that you will be able to change that all at once, but if you see the importance of making a commitment to establish and deepen friendships, it can make a big difference. It is best to begin with people you already know and have some friendly feelings about and to ask yourself who you think you might like to be closer to and who you feel you might come to trust with the more sensitive issues and vulnerable feelings of your life. One woman, going through a prolonged and painful process of breaking up, was told by the friend she shared her problems with, "I'm glad I can be there for you, but I'm not enough. Look around at the people you know and see who else you may want as a friend, and then pursue it. If you call four, three will probably want to get to know you better." She did call four, and all four were delighted to get together with her for lunch, dinner, etc. As she got to know them, she found that all had gone through similar situations of breaking bad relationships, and one was in the same position she was in at that moment. So her network expanded, and it was a bulwark against despair and against being pulled back to the destructive tie.

In making or deepening friendships, it can be useful to notice all your old discomforts about being close to people and to challenge the Beliefs on which they may be based, Beliefs such as "Nobody really cares," "Everyone is only out for himself," "Never

trust anyone outside the family," "Never trust anyone," "I have nothing to offer," "People will always
reject me," etc. Although you may once have had good
reason to learn these old Beliefs, as long as you operate on the basis of them, it will be that much harder to
break your addictive tie because it will mean entering
a world of unfriendly strangers all alone.

Not all of your friends will be equally helpful in
the addiction-breaking process. For example, there
may be some who run away from emotion-laden issues and only want to keep things superficial and
light. You had better not "recruit" them into the network of people you can lean on when the going gets
rough. If you make the mistake of trying to count on
those people, you may be let down. It would be too
bad if you concluded from this that *nobody* can be
counted on rather than that this one person has limitations. And even such a friend, though you may not
be able to share your turmoil, may be someone you
would want to turn to when you just want to lighten
your mood, get some relief from the heavy emotions
you may feel. In general, you will want to choose
friends who know what you are going through and
who really want to be supportive with the hardships
of getting out of a relationship.

The Specific Uses of Friendship
Overall, friends are simply there for you in a caring and supportive way, and that is the most important thing. But there are some specific ways friends
can be helpful in breaking an addiction.

*1. Helping You to Decide Whether You Want to
Leave.* In that often difficult decision, "should I stay
or should I go," there are three things you need from
your friends: objectivity, honest feedback, and a sense
that they will stand by you no matter what your decision. Eileen, when in the throes of her decision about
whether to leave Peter, said:

I knew I couldn't trust Hedi when she would tell me to get rid of Peter because I feel she hates all men and sees herself and all women as victims. But when Madge and Penny urged me to end it, I knew they were being objective. They both have good relationships with men, and I have no doubt that they would stand by me no matter what I decided.

If you are going to seek the help of your friends in deciding whether to end a relationship, it is important not only that they be honest but that you be honest in communicating to them what goes on in the relationship and your own conflicting feelings as fully and fairly as possible. It is no time to let shame, embarrassment, guilt, or fear of what your friend may think or may advise stand in the way.

2. *Helping You to Remember Why You Wanted to Leave.* Two days after Eileen left Peter for the first time she called her friend Madge at 1 A.M. and cried, "All I know is that I'm in hell, and I can't for the life of me remember why I've ended it with Peter. I can only remember how wonderful it was to be with him. What was wrong with it?" For a moment Madge was astonished, but then she remembered from her own experience of ending an unhappy affair how it is possible, in the rush of desperate anxieties, to totally erase the negatives, to completely lose sight of the things that led you to decide to get out. So she answered, "Eileen, how soon you forget! You don't remember all the times you called me and you were so hurt you could barely talk or so furious you wanted to kill him? You don't remember all the times he didn't call, all the times he didn't show up? And the time he took you away for a weekend and then deposited you in a motel room while he went to business conferences all day? And how you could ride with him in the car for two hours without his saying a word?" Et cetera. Eileen listened to these words and struggled to re-

member, as if she were trying to recall a fading dream. And she did remember—enough to get her through another few days without going back to Peter, although it would still be awhile before she could make a final break. But her call to Madge and Madge's response illustrates one of the primary ways friends can be helpful during this period—as a memory bank that, like a home computer, can play back to you data that you have stored there and that has been obscured by your Attachment Hunger's narrow aim.

Throughout the process of your disengagement, your friends can serve as a reality check in many ways, reminding you what they have seen about the relationship, telling you what they see you doing, keeping you from fooling yourself, challenging your tendencies to overvalue him and disparage yourself, and poking holes in your rationalizations for returning. In this role your friends can be a royal pain, but that's what friends are for.

3. *Rebuilding Your Identity.* Breaking a relationship, or even contemplating breaking it, can be an identity shattering experience. You became addicted largely because of feelings that, by yourself, you were incomplete, inadequate, unworthy, and insubstantial. Perhaps within the relationship you felt whole and effective and solid, but only in the context of that bond. The relationship, therefore, most likely reinforced the feeling and the Belief that as a separate entity you are not much, if anything. It is terrifying to think of taking a step toward becoming a nothing, and even *more* terrifying to actually take that step. In that situation, friends can be almost life saving. They can act as many mirrors, reflecting you back to yourself in your many aspects. They can be walls for you to hit up against to help you know your boundaries. They can talk back and yell back, showing you your impact. They can themselves be needy, reminding you that you have something to give. They can indicate that they value you, teaching you or reteaching you that

you are valuable. In short, they can give you precious proof that apart from your addictive relationship, you exist and that you have shape, substance, wholeness, and worth.

When I first mentioned Ben, the young man who spoke of feeling "like a nobody, kind of a wraith who drifts through the streets and has no clear form or purpose," I mentioned the helpfulness of his friend's response. Both the friend and his wife saw Ben as a very definite and valued person. But Ben remained depressed. He felt that without Helena, his lost Attachment Fetish Person, he was identityless, formless, and of no real interest to anyone. At first he reached out to his friends, but at one point he became reclusive, and his friends, in great concern, took the initiative in contacting him. Later, he spoke of this period:

> Sometimes I resented their calling and disturbing my retreat, but I also was aware in some dim way that they cared, that I had some meaning for them even though I was no longer attached to Helena. . . . A turning point happened one night when I was feeling particularly worthless, and I got a call from Nat who said, "Look, I know you've been feeling lousy, but try to pull yourself together for a few minutes because I need your help with something." And I did help him with this problem he was having. I mean I *knew*, I *could tell* that I was really being helpful, that what I said was damn smart advice. I got off the phone and felt, there must be a me there somewhere.

4. *Supporting You during Withdrawal.* You have all seen movies or TV shows in which the junkie or alcoholic is going through the pains, the tremors, the terror of withdrawal and about how nearly indispensable is the support of those who hold him, calm him, and encourage him through this nightmare. The withdrawal symptoms following the breakup of an addictive relationship are seldom that acute, but the suffering can be just as intense and often more pro-

longed. And it can be as important for those suffering withdrawal from a person to have the support, the reassurance and the holding as for those withdrawing from a substance.

Earlier (chapter 4) I wrote of Norma's horrifying weekend of withdrawal in which she found herself howling, and she set down on paper her feelings of being unmoored and floating off into space. I indicated that although she chose to go through her ordeal all alone, that she was part of a group of four women, four friends, who had formed a small network to help each other in difficulties they were having in their love relationships and that their presence in her mind during her self-imposed isolation was sustaining and comforting. At a different time, Maureen, another member of this foursome, was trying to kick her habit, which took the form of her relationship with a married man, Brad, who made it clear that he intended to stay married. One night (and the nights are often the worst time), a short while after she had told Brad that it was all over, Maureen was in a state of extreme agitation and despair. Her "network" knew she had ended it with Brad—they had been encouraging her to do it for a long time—and each of the women had told her she could call any time that she needed to talk. On this particular night, before she could call, Joette, the married member of the group, called her. She found Maureen sobbing. Maureen had had a few glasses of wine, trying to anesthetize her pain, but she was neither drunk nor anesthetized. "My only two real choices," she wept, "are to kill myself or keep seeing Brad. I simply don't have the strength to be alone, and I don't have any real faith any more that I will find someone else. There's been too many years, too many failures." Joette said:

> Listen, Maureen, you're in terrible pain, but I promise you it will pass and that you won't always feel this way. It's a natural part of the withdrawal. Your

whole perspective about time and about yourself is screwed up. And there are men out there whom you've never met who will become important in your life if you don't mess it up by killing yourself or getting back with that creep Brad.

They talked for over half an hour, and Maureen was in much better shape, much calmer, and able to joke a bit about her distress. But about two hours after that, Maureen called Joette. Obviously she had consumed more wine and was slurring her words and saying, "I'm going to call Brad's wife and tell her everything and tell her Brad really loves me and is only staying with her out of guilt, and she should let him go," etc. Again, Joette calmed her and said, "I'd come over, but I can't leave the kids alone and Cal isn't home. Call Norma or Kiki or I will." Maureen said she would, but Joette didn't trust the shape she was in and called the others herself. They both called Maureen, said they were coming over and they did. Both of them held her while she sobbed, helped her to collect her scattered feelings and thoughts, and kept her away from both the wine and the phone. Then the three of them sat around talking, sharing stories of being in similar straits, laughing at the absurdity of it all, bringing reality into Maureen's infant-dominated emotional state. After a while, Kiki, whose humor helped enormously, went home, but Norma stayed the night. There were a few times in the next few days when Maureen had to call one or the other of them when she was upset, but the main withdrawal crisis was over.

5. *Aiding Your Re-Entry.* Once the withdrawal symptoms have abated, you will have to face the problem of entering the social world as a separate and unattached individual. Here your friends can be helpful in two ways: giving you support during periods of discouragement and withdrawal-symptom flashbacks and helping to smooth your way to restructuring your

life. Over the next few months, Maureen called one or the other of her network when she felt particularly dejected or anxious or lonely. And, in addition, she and Norma enrolled in an art class that met one evening a week and at times met for dinner; she and Kiki went to several "singles" activities that she probably would not have gone to by herself; Joette arranged for her to meet some of her husband's single friends, and these four women continued to meet on a fairly regular basis to talk about issues important to them and just to have each other's companionship. It was enormously helpful to Maureen, and before a year was over she was developing a relationship with a caring and available man she met when she and Kiki attended a tennis party—a man she would not have met if she were still involved with Brad, or without the support of these friends.

Preparing Your Friends

Preparing your friends to help you is just as important as deciding which friends to turn to for support in breaking your addiction. That does not mean that it must be a "formal" preparation, a handbook of rules and instructions, any more than your network need be formal. But it does mean that it will be important that certain things get communicated:

1. That you are planning to break up your relationship (and here you may want feedback from them about this decision) and that you expect it will be a difficult and painful thing to do.
2. That the relationship you are ending is *an addiction* and that you might get depressed, panicky, confused, desperate, and feel driven to re-attach to your addictive person.
3. That what you need (depending on your evaluation of what a given friend could best offer) might be someone to:

210

(a) Listen to me and understand what I'm going through.

(b) Remind me that the awful feelings I'm going through will pass, and I'll feel okay again.

(c) Remind me that I can live without this person.

(d) Affirm that I am okay, whole, worthwhile, likable, and lovable, even without this person.

(e) Reassure me that he is not a one-and-only, is not the world's biggest bargain, and that I will not be alone forever.

(f) Keep me from calling him or seeing him—an impulse I will inevitably have during the withdrawal.

Again, depending on your feelings about a particular friend, you can decide what you can specifically request. At one point Maureen asked Norma to call her every night because "when I'm caught up in the depression, I may avoid calling you, maybe because I feel like a drag, or maybe I want to get so crazy that I can use it as an excuse to call Brad." So you have to decide whether to ask of your friends: Would you call me every night? Is it okay for me to call you when I need to? Is it okay for me to call in the middle of the night? Can you meet me for a drink some evenings after work? Will you remind me why I'm stopping this relationship if I forget? Do you know some party or something I can go to so I don't drive myself nuts? Et cetera. And you have to give your friends the right to participate as much or as little in your withdrawal network as they feel comfortable in doing. One man, knowing that the symptoms hit him with full force in the wee hours, asked three of his friends if he could call during the night if he felt the need. Two said no (one saying he had a crucial week in his work life coming up, and it was essential that he be well rested; the other saying the woman he was living with was ill, and it wouldn't be good to have her awakened), and one said "of course." At first this man felt let down and upset, a dangerous state because he felt that if nobody else cares he might as well go back to the one person to whom he felt connected. Then he was able to see that the two friends who said no were supportive in other ways, and he decided, "When it comes to being up to getting called in the middle of the night, I guess one out of three isn't so bad."

I am not proposing that it is impossible to break an addictive relationship without the help of a friend or friends, but the very nature of the Attachment Hunger level of the tie will make the experience easier and more likely to succeed if you call upon the power of friendship.

17

ADDICTION-BREAKING TECHNIQUES: OTHER USEFUL APPROACHES

One thing is for certain—the stronger your sense of having your own unique and valuable identity, the less subject you will be to being controlled by your Attachment Hunger. Your Attachment Hunger is a hangover from that early time when you were not a viable entity unless you were connected to someone else. So the more you can deepen your awareness that you are now a separate, adequate, and complete Self, the less you will fall prey to the infant feeling that you *must* be attached in order to survive physically or psychologically. There are techniques that can help you to become acquainted with your Self, that firm your grasp of the truth that you exist and have a singular and worthy identity.

CORE IDENTITY TECHNIQUES

Repairing damage to the foundations of your sense of Self, damage that may have occurred early in your life, is a difficult task, but it is the most important task you could possibly undertake. There may be limits determined by your early history, but these limits need not keep you from discovering and strengthening your feelings of wholeness, effectiveness, and worth. Mostly it is a matter of tuning in to the messages from within you—your feelings, images, and wishes—with understanding, with caring, and without condemnation. Here are some exercises that may help you to maintain a sense of who you are and of your value as an unattached person.

Sentence Completion
Previously (chapter 5) I wrote of how Eileen used the technique of completing part-sentences as a way of defining who she is without Peter. Below are some incomplete sentences that, if you finish them spontaneously and frankly, will put you in touch with basic aspects of your Self. You can set down one or more completions for each sentence.

I am
The main thing about me is
I always
I feel most like me when
What I like most about a person is
I will be
I get angry when
I feel happiest when
I believe in
One thing I want to accomplish is
What I like most about myself is
I hate it when
I was
I feel least like me when

I feel weakest when
I never
When I feel angry I
On a rainy day I like to
I feel good when I remember
When I'm alone I feel
Most of all I really want
I was the type of child who
One thing I'd like to change about myself is
I feel strongest when
On a beautiful day I like to
My favorite pastime is
When I feel happy I like to
If my relationship with ———— were to end

After you have completed these sentences, read them over. What type of person emerges? Keep in mind that even though you may not like the way you finished some of these sentences, the person who did finish them is you—that there *is a self* who has feelings, opinions, inclinations, and desires. You have an identity. And if there are aspects of that identity you do not like, instead of condemning yourself there are two other things you can do. You can be understanding toward yourself and about how you came to be who you are. And you can make it your goal to begin the arduous but rewarding work of changing yourself. You can make it your goal that if you complete these sentences a year from now, you will like the person reflected in those sentences more.

Body Awareness

Your Self is not a disembodied entity. How you feel about who you are is related in many ways to your sense of the size, the shape, and the functioning of your body. Suffering from the ending of a long love affair, Ben told a friend, "I feel like a nobody. . . ." He was describing a feeling people often have when they are unattached and particularly when an attachment is just broken—a feeling that they are *no body*. Any exercises that help you become aware of your own body—what it looks like, feels like, how it operates, its impact on its surroundings, and the world's impact on it—can enhance your feelings that there is a central core that is unmistakably your own and is a part of your unique identity. If you are a person who engages in sports or other active pursuits, it is a matter of tuning in to your own body in action and seeing it as a manifestation and reflection of who you are. But whether you are active or sedentary, the most basic physiological process that you can easily become aware of is your breathing. If you tend to lose touch with who you are when you are not connected to someone else, it can be helpful to spend some time each day doing deep breathing. When you can be alone and undisturbed, lie flat on your back on the floor or a firm bed. If you have difficulty letting your body relax, you can begin with the exercise of tensing different muscle groups and then letting them go. Start by tensing one leg as tightly as you can, holding it till it just begins to get painful, and then suddenly let it go limp. Then, in turn, tighten and relax your other leg, your hips and buttocks, your abdomen, your chest, your arms, and your neck and head muscles. When you feel that your body is relaxed, begin the deep breathing. First, inhale very slowly and deeply. Try to feel that you are breathing so deeply that the air is going down into your abdomen. Put your fingertips lightly on your abdomen below your navel. You know you are inhaling deeply if you can feel your abdomen rise. Hold the air briefly, then exhale very slowly through your mouth, even slower than the inhale. Keep repeating this and get into an easy rhythm. As you do, try to be aware of all your sensations, of the boundaries of your body, and how your body interacts with its surroundings. At what point is the air part of the outside world, and at what point is it part of your body? Let yourself sense that this is *you* breathing, *you* engaged in a basic life function that you have been doing since your birth cry. Your breathing is not dependent on your attachment to any other person. It is totally autonomous. It is a function of your physical, living, unique, and basic Self.

Core Fantasies

A few months after the relationship ended that left him feeling like a "wraith," Ben attended a workshop given by Dr. Daniel Malamud in which one of the exercises guided the participants step by step on a fantasy trip that led them to imagine and experience their own centers.* Afterward, in telling me of this experience Ben said:

> I saw as my center this huge room in Mammoth Cave with the most colorful stalactites and stalagmites. But I didn't feel it was empty because it was filled with light and humming. I could see and feel the pulsing energy, I could experience all those ricocheting atoms and whirling electrons. I had a deep sense of my own vitality and of who I am when you get down to basics.

In the later stage of his withdrawal from Ginny, the woman with whom he had long been involved, he let himself get in touch with his center "cave" again and at the same time made himself think "I will never see Ginny again." Though this thought still made him feel a bit shaky, the hum went on reassuringly, telling him of his core and keeping him from feeling like that ectoplasmic "wraith."

Derived directly from Daniel Malamud's workshop exercises, there is a way that can help you to get in touch with the sense of a core or center of your

---

* The instructions I will give here are an adaptation I've made from an exercise developed by Daniel I. Malamud, Ph.D., of New York City, as part of his Psychosynthesis Seminars, given first on October 15, 1971. The particular seminar from which this was derived is called The Second Chance Family.

selfhood and to discover more about it. As with the deep breathing, get your body into a comfortable position and a relaxed state. When you feel relaxed, fix your attention on some object in the room—a chair, a lamp, a picture—that you will return to after your fantasy trip. Look at it. Imprint it on your mind. That will be your home base point. Then close your eyes, and imagine that there is a place in you that is your center, a center that is uniquely yours, a core of your being, your awareness, your energy, and your wisdom. Try to locate it. Where in you is it? What does it look like? Let yourself look at this inner area for a while. Then picture that this inner area, this center, is becoming filled with light, becoming more and more visible. The lighter it gets, the more clearly you can see what this center looks like. And not only can you see it, but you can hear a hum emanating from it. A hum of pure energy. Let yourself hear it. Let yourself be aware that this hum is coming from your center. After a while you can diminish the hum, but try to maintain an awareness of the center it is coming from, how it sounds and what it looks like. Hold onto the awareness that what you are hearing and seeing is your unique core. When you have a firm sense of that core, begin to let your thoughts come back to the room you are in. Begin to picture the object you chose as your home base point. Then slowly open your eyes and look at your home base point, letting yourself know that your trip to your center is over but that you've brought back a sense of it that you will try to keep with you. Stretch your body and sit up.

You can probably create your own way of seeing, hearing, exploring, and being in touch with your own unique center. Some people I know have drawn pictures of it, sculpted it, and written about it. The method is less important than the message it brings. That message is that *you do have an identity that is real, complete, and yours alone.* You may have feelings to the contrary—that your identity is weak or cloud-like or fragmented—but these feelings distort the fact that you are a solid and whole person. Any feelings of insubstantiality you may have are coming from a time early in your childhood when your sense of a separate and independent self was very shaky and just getting formed. But now your identity does not depend on being connected to another person. In fact, being connected in an addictive way to another person, though giving you the *illusion* of identity, is a sure way to further weaken your sense of who you, as a separate being, really are.

Awareness of Wanting

Having a sense of a solid core means knowing what you want. Many people have a deficient sense of what they want and become very dependent on other people to tell them what they want. Even as I write those words I am struck by the paradox: that another person should tell me *what I want* is a contradiction in terms. Yet some people lead their lives that way. We accept it when a little child in a candy store asks, faced with an array of goodies, "Mommy, what candy do I want?" But it is not as becoming when an adult in a restaurant looks at the menu and asks his partner, "What dessert do I want?" And sometimes these questions refer to needs and decisions deeper and much wider in their ramifications than the choice of a dessert. If your sense of self is shaky in a way that is reflected in not knowing what you want, I would like to suggest a little exercise taken from one that the psychoanalyst and group leader Ruth Cohn (formerly of New York, now in Switzerland) prescribed for some of her patients. Take ten minutes of each day in which you can arrange to be undisturbed and simply give yourself the task: In these ten minutes I will focus entirely on what I want at this given moment, what my body wants to do, what my thoughts want to do, and to as great an extent as possible, I will do what I want." This is not as easy as it may sound, particularly if you are not used to being tuned in to what you want. You may find some of your wants are unclear, that you are paralyzed by conflicting wants (like wanting to get some ice cream from the freezer versus wanting not to gain weight) or by feeling you don't want anything. But the fact is, you do have wants with which, for reasons of your history, you are not sufficiently in touch. Many children are brought up to believe that it is wrong, sinful, and self-indulgent to want something for themselves and learn early to repress their awareness of their wants. To be able to get in touch with your wanting self becomes a path to discovering your identity. This does not mean embarking on a life of hedonistically and irresponsibly pursuing each whim or desire, but recognizing your wanting self as a vital part of you so that you can then decide, in context of the whole picture, what it is best for you to do. This will firm up your sense of your center so that you will not need to be attached to someone else in order to "know" what you want. And this will make it easier to break with that someone else if that is what you want to do.

Thought Stopping and Distraction

Eileen told me, "I found a way to think of Peter a lot less often. I wear this rubber band around my wrist, and as soon as I notice thoughts of Peter intruding into my mind, I pull the rubber band out and let it snap against my wrist hard. It really works!" At first I was appalled at this effort to condition herself *not to think* about Peter through punishment. The basis of my own approach is that the addiction is best stopped through a lot of thinking about it in the form of recognizing its infant nature and using this recognition to keep Attachment Hunger from dominating. To short cut this process with a behavioral gimmick seemed clearly to be too easy a solution. It might help a person break his connection to a particular person, but if he learned nothing about its roots and its working, it could well doom him to keep repeating the pattern with others and be left with nothing but very sore wrists. I still believe that this position is absolutely valid—to conquer the addiction you must make profound changes in your sense of self, in your attachment needs, and in your self-defeating ways of getting these needs gratified.

But then I realized that Eileen had developed a very deep understanding of the needs, patterns, and history that went into forming her attachment to Peter and other similar men before him, and that she had strengthened her sense of her worth and viability as a separate person. In that context, her behavioral gimmick was not a *substitute* for real change but *a useful technique* in dealing with the residue of her attachment—the intruding thoughts about Peter. I could see that it had great value in severing the last vestigial ties to him. And I could see the appropriateness of recommending some behavioral techniques as *part* of the process of breaking an addiction.

Dr. Deborah Phillips has written about several types of such behavioral techniques in a book designed to help people "to get over a relationship that's ended."* The gimmick Eileen used would be one method of "thought stopping" that is recommended by Dr. Phillips, although she indicates that often just yelling aloud the word "stop" when thoughts of your lost love begin is enough to begin to diminish the frequency of these thoughts. (Of course, you had better be alone when you yell, or you might find yourself with other problems.) She also suggests you might keep a record of the frequency of these thoughts so you can note how it tapers off. To aid in the thought stopping, it can be helpful first to make a list of some

* Deborah Phillips, *How To Fall Out of Love* (Boston: Houghton Mifflin, 1978).

221

of the most pleasant things you can think of and to practice imagining them in some detail. Then, when the unwanted thoughts of your lover intrude, besides loudly or silently yelling "stop" or snapping a rubber band, you can focus your thoughts instead on the pleasant image, distracting your mind from its obsessive and wasteful preoccupation.

How does such "thought stopping" and distraction fit into the context of deepening your self-awareness and your understanding of your feelings and their origins that I have advocated throughout the book? I have even suggested that you take the time to be alone and to let yourself go into the black pit of your pain and your despair (as did Norma in chapter 4). I have recommended exploring the earliest beginnings of such feelings, of seeing the influence of the Attachment Hunger level on your current life. Isn't that just the opposite of now saying, "Stop thinking about it"?

Yes, it is. But the point is, there is a time to think about it and a time not to think about it, and each can be valuable and appropriate if the use of it makes sense in the total picture. If you stop yourself from thinking about the other person and the meaning of your getting into an addicted relationship with him before you have had a chance to understand it, you will learn nothing from the experience, making it highly likely that you will enter into another such relationship. But to continue to obsess about the relationship even after you have understood it and have used your knowledge to strengthen your identity as a separate person serves no further constructive purpose. At that point, it makes sense to use whatever techniques may be helpful to end this preoccupation and free you for other things.

The same point may be made in regard to other behavior modification techniques recommended by Dr. Phillips, such as silently ridiculing your partner by imagining him in an absurd or degrading light. While it may well be worth using these techniques if you sense that they would be helpful to you, I would again caution that they are a supplement to and not a substitute for the basic task of understanding your addiction and using this understanding to enhance your capacity to be a confident, complete, and worthy person even when you are free from your current partner or from *any* addictive attachment.

Multiple Attachments

Attachment Hunger is not an aberration but part of our human heritage. At times there may clearly be too much of it, or it may be of such strength and intensity that it propels our actions against our own best interest. But in all of us, even where it is not wildly out of control, there is an irreducible amount of Attachment Hunger that stays with us from infancy, and there are some ways of dealing with it that are better than others. One obviously better way, as seen in many places throughout this book, is to avoid putting all your attachment needs in one basket. Perhaps the greatest devastation a person can feel is when he has placed all his needs for closeness, connection, nurturance, and identity in one person, and then loses that person. This is not saying that there isn't particular value in there being a prime commitment, a primary life-sharing person, but having a close relationship with one such person at the expense of other attachments and commitments besides being risky is very narrowing. Stanton Peele puts it this way:

> Adults in natural settings whose lives revolve around only one focus are in an unstable, precarious position. The behavior this leads to, either in clinging to the one object or in bewailing its loss, is a serious disruption of the living psyche. The difference between having one connecting point to the world and many (at a given

time) *is a difference of degree that amounts to a difference in kind.* *

Peele is implying that if we have many rather than one "connecting point to the world," it decreases our dependence on that one, which in turn makes us feel less vulnerable and limited. If we have multiple sources of gratification of our needs for love, nurturance, and stimulation, we will be more secure, independent, and free to be ourselves. This does not mean that all our attachments will have equal meaning. It is not only possible but highly desirable to be deeply devoted to your primary partner and still have much of your need for connectedness met by friends, close kin, colleagues, co-workers, and others.

Connecting with the Timeless
There is another source of connectedness that does not involve specific other people and that has some advantages that attachments to people do not. The Gershwin song expresses the romantic wish that though "the Rockies may tumble, Gibraltar may crumble, they're only made of clay, but—Our love is here to stay." Well, the Rockies and Gibraltar are still around while countless people who earnestly sang these lyrics to their partner are not. Or their partner is not. Or both, through separation or death, are gone.

I am not proposing that it is better to love rocks than people. But I am implying two other propositions: (1) that it is unrealistic not to recognize the possibility of any relationship being transient and ephemeral, and (2) that the more we can root some of our attachment needs in things more lasting and even timeless, the firmer is the ground on which we stand in life's changes and discontinuities. Perhaps I used

* Stanton Peele, *Love and Addiction* (N.Y.: Signet, 1975), p. 224. (Emphasis added.)

the lyric of the Gershwin song because it is so connected in my mind with an experience a friend told me. He had begun to recover from the distress and depression that followed the ending of his marriage, and he decided to drive with a friend to visit the Grand Canyon, Bryce Canyon, Yosemite, and other wonders he long had wanted to see. For the first week or so, his depression returned with greater intensity than in many months. He could think only of the lovely sights he and his ex-wife had shared in happier days, and how he had always hoped to take this trip with her and his children. His sadness became so great that he thought he would have to cut the trip short and return home.

> But then I saw the sun come up on the Grand Tetons. Those colors. The incredible magnificence of those peaks. The air so clean that you could see every detail for miles. And this time, instead of feeling alone and sorry for myself, I felt thrilled with the world and that I was part of it. I realized the grandeur of it, but instead of it making me feel puny it made me bigger. And I continued the trip and I communed with the redwoods and the Pacific and the cliffs at Big Sur. . . . I can't always hold onto the feeling, but I know it's there, and when I get in touch with it, I don't feel empty or fragmented off.

The Grand Tetons did not replace his lost relationship with his wife, but they provided another point of attachment to something deeply nurturant once he allowed himself to take it in. Many people find strength, bliss, awe, and feeling of being part of something greater in the splendors of nature, and these reactions may satisfyingly re-create some of the experience of the early fusion. Others find that the grandness of it all, be it the majesty of the Rockies or the infinite distances of the Milky Way, helps them to

225

gain a more realistic perspective about being without a particular partner or being without any primary person for a while.

There are many avenues for feeling an attachment to the timeless. For some, like my friend, it may be in experiencing the wonder of breathtaking landscapes or the unending suns and vast spaces of the cosmos. For others it is their sense of *connection with all living things*. For others it is their sense of *kinship with all mankind*. And for many it takes the form of communing with *their concept of a Supreme Being,* either through formal religious doctrine and ritual or through their own conceptualization of a higher power. When someone who has ended or lost a love relationship is able to feel "I am not alone because God loves me," he may be in touch with some of his earliest experiences of being loved and protected. When he feels "I am one of God's creatures" or "I am part of a greater plan," he re-experiences some of the earliest feelings of family, and he feels less alone.

You cannot and should not try to coerce yourself into believing in a "higher power" if you do not believe it, or to find solace and gratification in nature or the cosmos or your fellow creatures if, in truth, they do not much interest you. But you can make the effort to open yourself up to a wide range of phenomena and experiences that will expand your boundaries and increase your points of contact with potential sources of Attachment Hunger satisfaction. Perhaps for you, the source of attachment gratifications that are less ephemeral and limited than a single relationship may reside in a deep and personally significant *commitment to values* you respect and cherish, such as love or compassion or the pursuit of knowledge or the seeking of wisdom or the betterment of the lot of your fellow man. Feeling connected to such values can make you feel less isolated and insignificant. Such commitments not only may meet some of your attachment needs in a socially constructive way, but they reduce your dependence on the vicissitudes of any one relationship for feeling connected, whole, and worthwhile. Or perhaps you might find that you need to lean less heavily on your partner to help you to overcome feelings of emptiness and insignificance by being in touch with the well-springs of your own *creativity* and by developing its expression. In the exhilaration of creating you may experience some of the feelings of rapture and well-being of the early attachment period while at the same time you are experiencing a profound and essential aspect of your core that does not depend at all on your being attached to another person. What a happy paradox! (And by creating something that never existed before until you made it, you may glimpse the possibility that you can *re-create* your own life.) One woman, who always had an interest in painting, said:

When we broke up, for months I was too depressed to touch the watercolors. I had begun haunting the singles bars looking for a quick replacement, but it was all empty and stupid. Then I got back to sketching and painting, and suddenly I was into it with a passion I never felt before—I mean I'd plan to paint for an hour or two, and then four hours would be gone. Maybe Freud was right about sublimation! All I know is that besides the fact that I think I'm producing good stuff, it makes me so much less desperate about men. And if I can work on a painting to get it to express what I have in my mind, then maybe I can also work to make the kind of relationship I want with a man. . . .

Others may find more timeless and many-faceted attachments in the pursuit of *their own growth and development*. They may strive to be more wise, more spiritual, more truthful, more courageous, more knowledgeable, more skillful, or more loving. And as part of this, they may pursue a journey to their own core or center and come to cherish and value who they are. A person who does not experience his core said, "I feel like a nothing—unless I have someone." A person who can experience his core but dislikes it said, "I feel like I'm on a blind date with someone I don't like, and I have to be polite." A person who connects up with his core and likes it said, "I'm good company to myself, and while I am very happy with Joan, it's nice to know that if it doesn't work out, I'll still be with somebody I like."

As I said earlier, you cannot force yourself to take on beliefs and quests that feel artificial to you just because it may, like a placebo, make you feel better. But it is important to open yourself to a new awareness: *The fact is* that you do have a core that is all yours and that can be better known, developed, and cared about by you; *the fact is* that you are both alone and not alone—you have a connection with the people around you, your society, the world, the chain of life, and the cosmos. That is not a distortion, not a phony or pollyanna belief. *The distortion is* the Attachment Hunger level notion that without being attached to a particular other person you are alone and disconnected. To open yourself to being aware of and taking nourishment from the many connections you do have, both transient and timeless, is to be in touch with a much more mature reality than the infant-based concept of utter aloneness and bleakness without a certain someone. You may stubbornly fight to hold onto that infant-based view, because to give it up is to surrender a primal belief that you need this one attachment (Mommy and I are one) to exist and be happy, and to give up the hope of ultimately securing that blissful attachment. But if you can graduate to a more adult concept of your infinite connectedness, you will feel yourself to be bigger rather than smaller and to be freer rather than dependent on the cheap fix of an addictive relationship.

18

THE USES OF PSYCHOTHERAPY IN BREAKING THE ADDICTION

At what point would it be a good idea to see a psychotherapist for help with ending a bad relationship? In general, the answer is when you have not been able to end it despite long and hard efforts, and despite the attempt to use the kind of approaches I have indicated. More specifically, psychotherapy is called for when any of these four conditions exist:

1. When you know you are terribly unhappy in the relationship but you are unclear about whether in the cost/benefit ratio the price you are paying is too high and you are confused about whether you should accept it as it is, make further efforts to improve it, or get out of it.

2. When you have concluded that you should leave, are suffering a lot in remaining, know that you would be better off breaking it, have tried to get yourself to end it, but still remain stuck.

3. When you suspect that you are staying for the wrong reasons, like guilt or terrible fearfulness and insecurity about being unattached, and you have been unable to overcome the paralyzing effect of those feelings through your own efforts.

4. If you recognize that getting into and remaining in that kind of relationship is part of a repeated and self-defeating pattern that you have not been able to change.

When Eileen first consulted me, she was a terribly unhappy woman with many physical symptoms that her internist had suggested were due to tension and stress. It was no secret to her what the tension and stress was about. In the first few minutes of the very first session, she said, "I'm in love with a guy who treats me like dirt much of the time." In response to my inquiry, she indicated she had made many efforts to communicate her dissatisfactions to Peter and to ask for changes in his way of relating to her, but to no avail. So I asked her why she stayed in the relationship, and she gave me some of the self-deceiving reasons that I reported in the first chapter: "It's not that he doesn't love me. He's just afraid of commitment." And, "He loved me once, and it just doesn't disappear. He has to love me." The treatment really began with my questioning these rationales. "Why can't it be true that he doesn't love you?" "Even if he does love you, what difference does that make if he is afraid of commitment and treats you badly?" You may need this kind of dogged confrontation with reality from someone else because it can be so hard to stop deluding yourself, and to stop denying the evidence of your own eyes and ears when you have an addictive stake in holding onto the relationship. And so it can be a very useful function of psychotherapy to help you see the relationship honestly and without distortion, and thus make it more likely that your decision to remain with it or to leave it is reality based.

Eileen fought hard, for a while, not to see the truth of her relationship with Peter, but when she could dare to look at it with clarity, she knew she would have to end it. She could see that the cost to her self-respect, her emotions, and her health was too high relative to the few crumbs of good feelings that she derived from it. When she still balked about ending it, she had to face the real reasons, reasons that dwelled deep within her, for hanging onto Peter.

Besides helping you to face the reality of your situation and to decide whether it is best to remain in the relationship or not, psychotherapy, by focusing on your underlying motives for staying in a relationship that is bad for you, can help you to understand why you are doing what you are doing. It can help you not only to see but to feel that you are transferring very early needs, feelings, and patterns of behavior into the present in a way that is self-defeating. And this type of awareness can have a double value: It can help you to leave the bad relationship in which you are currently ensnared, and it can help you to keep yourself from automatically repeating the same pattern with someone else.

Eileen learned much about her insecurity and her desperate yearning to be attached to someone. She could see how her attachment needs gained strength and tenacity by being frustrated too much, too early, both by her mother, who was rarely sensitively tuned in to her needs and emotions, and by her father who would give her periodic loud and exciting bursts of attention when he arrived home from his merchant marine journeys but who would then retreat, leaving her feeling that she must have failed to please him or he wouldn't withdraw and wouldn't go away again. In short, she got in touch with the inexorable longings of her ungratified Attachment Hunger and how she was seeking, in her current relationships, to find the security, wholeness, identity, and sense of worth that she never derived from her relationship with her parents. And this enabled me to pose to her these questions:

> If you want that loving support you never had, then why are you trying to get it from someone like Peter? There are many men in the world who would be much more loving and supportive than he is; how come you've never permitted yourself to have a relationship with a man like that? Why do you have a history of relationships with men who have the same defect in giving that Peter has and who make you feel worse about yourself rather than better?

In focusing on this and probing her thoughts and feelings Eileen came to the crucial insight I wrote of earlier (chapter 6).

> When I meet a nice warm guy who obviously likes me, it usually turns me off. Maybe I don't trust it because I never had it, or maybe I don't feel I deserve it, but I often think of him as a namby pamby or even a jerk. . . . You see, it's not just the loving I want, it's to get it from some hard-nosed bastard, someone as ungiving and cold as my parents. What I'm hooked into is the challenge of melting stones.

Eileen could increasingly experience the absurd but deadly futility of this task.

It was not these insights alone that enabled Eileen to eventually break both her addiction to Peter and her overall addiction to ungiving men. A crucial element in this was the therapeutic repair work of her damaged sense of self, a repair work that took many forms of self-exploration and of her taking risks with new behavior. My support of these processes enabled changes to slowly appear and become a firm part of her. Perhaps the most important part of the therapy at this point was not so much in the accuracy of my interpretations or the soundness of my guidance, but in Eileen's awareness that I knew her deeply and that I respected and liked her. She also could see that I encouraged and supported her efforts to become her own person. There was something healing in her awareness of my caring, something that enabled her to begin to correct her old impaired core, confidence, and self-image.

After Eileen broke off with Peter she found to her surprise that she was no longer at all attracted to such ungiving men. In working out what had been keeping her with Peter she had resolved much of the basis for her addiction. But at this point a strange and unexpected thing happened—though she dated much warmer and more giving men, she treated them arrogantly and even cruelly. She made bitchy demands and attempted to control the relationship with imperiousness. The men either battled with her, left her, or capitulated, and if they did the latter, she used them contemptuously. At first we both believed her actions were motivated by years of stored up wishes to revenge herself on all the Peters who had ever mistreated her, and undoubtedly there was truth to this view, but her despotic treatment of the men in her life lessened only a little with this interpretation, and she made a shambles of several relationships that had real promise. One day as I listened very carefully to what she was saying, trying to determine whether there was some element I was missing, I caught a glimpse of what it was, and I made this interpretation:

It's not simply that you want revenge on those self-centered, domineering, and ungiving men, but that there has always been a hidden side to you that is very much like them. Most of your life you were at the receiving end of such treatment, but I think you secretly identified with men like Peter, that you were secretly being the aggressive bastard through him. Now you're feeling stronger, so the aggressive and sadistic you has come out into the open.

Eileen was momentarily startled, and then she laughed with that special guileless burst of laughter that often comes with sudden insight. "Right on," she said. "Right on."

This enabled us to work on what turned out to be the final stronghold of her self-defeating behavior with men, her tendency to feel that being aggressive and sadistic were the only ways to feel strong, safe, and adequate. She was able to move to a relationship with a giving man, a relationship that was reciprocally loving and mutually respectful. Clearly, for Eileen, therapy was helpful. This is not always true for a variety of reasons. But it is helpful often enough to make it well worth going into therapy when you are in an unhappy or destructive relationship and are having trouble unconnecting yourself from it, or even deciding whether you want to break it. You are much more likely to be able to make the best decision and to follow through on it with the help of a competent psychotherapist than without such help.

Addiction to Psychotherapy

If your reason to begin psychotherapy was at least in part to help you to break an addiction to your partner in a love relationship, there is definitely a danger that you could switch that addiction to the person of the therapist and to the process of the therapy. You are addicted to your partner in the first place because your Attachment Hunger has gained too great a position of control over your life. Your Attachment Hunger is not going to be immediately reduced or contained, so the need to depend on and fuse with another person is very likely to focus on a person who listens to you carefully, tunes in to who you are, tries to be helpful, and yet who is just unattainable enough to trigger that challenge to get whatever you felt you did not get enough of from your parents (or your current partner). This frequently happens, and it is often a helpful and perhaps even necessary part of the treatment for many people. We have seen with Eileen, for example, that her awareness of my concern and regard was an important element in repairing her fragile sense of self. There is no doubt that Eileen was, for a while, highly dependent on me and on her visits to me. I was an important transitional attachment, someone she could feel connected with as she broke other connections and other patterns. Often she would feel strong urges not to leave the office when the session was over. "Why can't I stay? Don't you care enough? What would you do if I don't leave?" If the therapy had become stuck right there, it would have been changing one addiction for another, like going from heroin to methadon, and who can say with certainty which is better?

Some critics of psychotherapy are so mindful of this danger that they see it as often outweighing the benefits of therapy. Stanton Peele admonishes:

> Therapy must mean releasing emotional energy, energy which has previously been blocked or misdirected, so that it can express itself constructively. When, instead, therapy diverts energy from real-life issues and relationships, it stands the danger of becoming an addiction. While becoming more dependent on the psychiatrist's approval (or mere presence) for sustenance, the patient may be sacrificing the opportunity and even any desire for other satisfactions.*

I couldn't agree more, but what is overlooked is that while the dependence on the psychotherapist is often real and strong, the aim of a competent ethical professional is to bring about the end of the dependence. Paradoxically, the formation of that dependence is often necessary for a person to coalesce his personality and restore his selfhood so that he can feel com-

* Stanton Peele, *Love and Addiction* (N.Y.: Signet, 1976), p. 168.

plete enough to end the dependence. In this sense, the job of the therapist is in some ways similar to the job of parent: to enable the dependent person to develop the strength and confidence to break away and become independent. Earlier I referred to the English psychoanalyst Winnicott who said that while it is the mother's job to "disillusion" the child (about her being an extension of him), she can never hope to succeed unless first she has given him some opportunity for illusion. This is often true about the psychotherapist's job as well, just as it is true of the job goals of teachers and mentors; in other words, the proper aim of all these professionals is to enable the person who comes to them to become strong enough and proficient enough to leave them. At times the process of leaving the therapist is difficult, painful, and enlightening. When Eileen, after several years in treatment, said in February that she thought she'd be ready to end therapy in July, I agreed that this seemed like a realistic timetable. Very soon after she fell into a mild depression. As we probed her feelings, she saw that even though *she* brought up the termination, she felt very rejected by my agreeing to it. "The least you could do was to put up a fight to keep me," she said, more in anger than in jest. We were then able to focus on her very mixed feelings about ending her therapy, about the conflict between her wishes to be independent and her wishes to remain snugly attached to me, and how that repeated the earliest of inner conflicts. There were rocky times in which she experienced a recurrence of anxiety attacks and even some of the rashes and other physical symptoms that ushered her into treatment, but I used these not to say, "Obviously you are still too troubled to leave," but to deepen our understanding of her ambivalence and to support her movement toward ending treatment and being autonomous.

When the therapist clearly sees his job as ending the dependent relationship and launching his patient, then the dependency on him is transitory, useful, and does not become another morbid addiction. At times, for a variety of motives, some therapists do not do this job well. Perhaps they do not fully appreciate the goal of launching the patient. Perhaps they are not too competent. Unfortunately, in some instances they may hold onto their patient for financial gain. But when the therapist is not sufficiently helpful in weaning his patient from dependence on him, the most frequent reason is his own unresolved emotional dependence on his patient. The patient's looking up to him for help and guidance may be too gratifying to easily give up; the closeness he may feel with the patient may satisfy some of his own Attachment Hunger needs; or he may simply be very fond of the patient and will miss seeing him regularly. Usually, when therapists are aware of these motivations, they are able to keep such motives from inappropriately interfering with the patient's progress toward termination. The trouble is, these motives are often unconscious and are rationalized with interpretations and injunctions such as: "You are trying to run away to avoid looking at feelings that are beginning to emerge"; "You are stopping prematurely so you can go back to your old patterns"; "There is much more work to do"; etc.

How are you to know—if you are the patient—when to seriously honor the therapist's opinion in this regard (because he will very often be right) and when he is rationalizing some need of his own to keep you from leaving? It is an extremely difficult differentiation to make. You are a bit ahead of the game simply to realize that such mixed motives on the part of your therapist are possible. And you would not be out of line to ask the therapist to examine whether there might be hidden needs to keep you there. But it is usually best to suspend judgment for a while and listen to the therapist very carefully, to give yourself the time and opportunity to determine if your wish to leave is some kind of resistance, sabotage, or flight.

If you feel you have examined your wish to leave

very thoroughly, have given yourself ample time to explore the nuances of your motives, and conclude (whether it's because you have achieved what you want or because the therapy is not helpful) that it really is time for you to go, then you will be facing some of the problems of breaking a tie to someone who does not want you to leave. You have to be able to keep firmly in mind that it is your life, not his, your decision to make, not his. If you find yourself feeling guilty about leaving, remember that it is your therapist's job to help you find your own way, and that if he has negative feelings about what you finally decide, it is his job to deal with them, not yours.

I recall when Ben began to say with increasing firmness that he was ready to leave, and I had some doubts and misgivings about the timing of it and what could have been some less-than-healthy motives for it, even though I knew that he had accomplished much of what he had set out to achieve in therapy. Then Ben said:

Look, I feel quite certain that the end of this month is the time for me to end treatment. It feels right, it makes sense, and one thing I've learned here is to trust my judgment more. Maybe you're right that it's a mistake. If so, I can always come back. But maybe you're wrong and have just come to so enjoy my fascinating dreams, great personality, and fantastic sense of humor that you don't want to let go. It's going to be tough leaving without your blessing, but I'm prepared to if I have to.

I looked at Ben. This was the man whose self had been so damaged that he felt "like a wraith drifting through the streets." I knew that he was right and I was wrong. He was ready to go.

19

APHORISMS TO BREAK AN ADDICTION BY

We have seen how you may maintain a battery of unfounded Beliefs, rationalizations, false hopes, and other self-deceptive ploys that can enable you to keep your addiction going despite the pain and despite the fact that, on another level, you may know better. I've prepared a list of antidotes to these distortions, a list of aphorisms custom-made to help you challenge those ideas that either you or your society have created that promote your addiction rather than help you diminish and control it. It might be helpful to take from this list the ones that you need most to help you counteract the ways of thinking that are keeping you stuck. Then write them down and tack them up or put them somewhere for ready reference.

239

ADDICTION-BREAKING APHORISMS

1. You *can* live without him/her (probably better).
2. Love is not enough (to make a good love relationship).
3. Limerence is not enough.
4. A love relationship is mutual and helps each partner feel *better* about himself, not worse.
5. Guilt is not reason enough to stay.
6. You don't have to love someone to be addicted to him.
7. Just because you're jealous doesn't mean you love him; you can be jealous of someone you can't stand.
8. What you see is what you get, so stop hanging on to the Belief you can change the other person.
9. Love doesn't necessarily last forever.
10. You can't always work it out, no matter how much you may want to.
11. Some people die of bad relationships. Do you want to be one of them?
12. If someone says, "I don't want to be tied down," "I'm not ready for a relationship," "I'm not going to leave my spouse," etc., *believe him*.
13. Half a loaf isn't better than none.
14. He/she doesn't *have to* love you.
15. It doesn't *have to* get better.
16. The pain of ending it won't last forever. In fact, it won't last nearly as long as the pain of not ending it.
17. If it will be the same way five or ten years from now, do you want it?
18. There will be anxiety, loneliness, depression when you end it, but these feelings will last for only a limited amount of time and then will stop.
19. You won't be alone forever; that's thinking in Infant Time.

20. It's never too late to make a change; the longer you wait, the more time wasted.

21. The intensity of your withdrawal symptoms does not indicate the strength of your love but the strength of your addiction.

22. You are a whole and valuable person apart from that relationship.

23. When you feel inadequate, incomplete, or worthless apart from him/her, childhood feelings are taking over.

24. He/she is not the "one and only."

25. If you end this bad relationship, you will be opening your life to new possibilities.

20

IS THERE LIFE
AFTER ADDICTION?

There are three kinds of questions I hear most commonly from people who are in the throes of breaking an addiction to a person:

1. Will I ever get over it? Even if I use my willpower to end it, can I ever really get him out of my system?
2. If I end it, will I be able to bear being alone? Can I ever feel all right about being on my own?
3. Will I ever have another love relationship? And why should it be better than what I have now?

These questions address the issue of what your life may be like when you end your relationship with your current partner. The underlying concern is whether there is life after addiction. But each question deserves a detailed response.

Will I Ever Get Over It?

Here are two examples from the lives of people we have come to know, Eileen (and Peter) and Jason (and Dee).

Months after Eileen ended her relationship with Peter he called asking if he could drop by and see her "for old times sake." Eileen was feeling a bit vulnerable because she had had a bad week in both her social and work life, so she said okay. She said:

> I think mostly I was testing myself to see if it was really over. I found that I felt nothing for him when I saw him. Where was the old attraction? I noticed that he had a paunch and small eyes and just wasn't as good-looking as he used to seem to me. I did go to bed with him, though. That was the real test, because I always felt that sex was very special with him. I remember telling you that I would never find anyone who could make love like Peter. Well, it was a big nothing. He's not a particularly good or tender lover. He works hard at it, but it's clear now that it's because his ego makes him have to make every woman feel he's the greatest. And I used to think it was because he loved me and was expressing it that way! After a while, I stopped him. I couldn't wait to get him out of there. When he left I didn't feel particularly sad or gloating. I felt kind of neutral. He's really out of my system now.

And Jason told me of running into Dee on a downtown street.

> She looked fabulous, and I felt a rush of the old feelings. I invited her to have lunch with me, and as we sat there talking, a strange thing began to happen. I saw her at a distance, as if I were watching a movie screen closeup of her face—and particularly her mouth. Her mouth rarely stopped talking, and it was all about her. No matter what I said, after I got out about two sentences, she would relate it to herself

243

somehow and start blabbing and babbling in the most incredibly Dee-centered way. And she put down everyone else with her famous scathing sarcasm that I once used to find so witty. Now it seemed boring and sick. Right before my eyes her prettiness became coarseness and emptiness, and finally ugliness. . . . I never believed I'd be saying this, but I hope I never see her again.

These examples illustrate that the addiction can be fully broken and the feelings completely changed, even when both the attraction (limerence) and the Attachment Hunger feelings were very strong. (In fact, when the feelings turn so much into their opposite, it's a good indication that addiction has been at work. Addiction is based on an illusion, and when the illusion goes, the inevitable disappointment and anger often paint the former beloved in pitilessly repugnant hues. This differs from most non-addictive close relationships which, when ended, frequently leave intact earlier feelings of friendship and warmth.) Both Eileen and Jason had worked hard to get to the point of such a total change in feelings. They had looked at their relationships with increasing candor and with heightened awareness of who they and the other persons were in the interaction. They did not suddenly turn off. It was the end point of a long journey of discovery and dis-illusion. And what is more important than the fact of their ending these relationships so completely is that while both Eileen and Jason for a while after felt some surge of attraction when meeting other people like Peter and like Dee, they went through stages of counteraddiction. First, they deliberately avoided involvement with these Attachment Fetish Persons because they knew it was bad for them. Next, they found that they were no longer attracted to such people. Finally, they felt repelled and "allergic." As Jason put it:

I was talking to a woman at a party. She had those flashing eyes and bubbly talkativeness that always hooked me. But this time I could hear what she was saying and watched what she was doing, and it all spelled "Me, Me, Me." This time I didn't let her looks and her ebullience keep me from seeing what she was really like and from knowing as clearly as if I had a crystal ball what a nightmare a relationship with her would be for me. I excused myself and fled.

This is the same Jason who, in his relationships with women, had been endlessly engaged in the futile and frustrating challenge of trying to get his cold and self-centered mother to be warm and loving. He had finally put down that task and began to move in more promising directions for his fulfillment.

What these examples also indicate is that breaking an addiction to a particular partner should *not*, at best, be an isolated and single act. It has its most lasting value as part of a larger process. The break should be part of a growing understanding of the way feelings and needs from that early time when you depended on others for everything have now caused you to attach yourself to another person. It should give you the insight that you have been deluding yourself that only through such an attachment could you feel complete, adequate, secure, worthwhile, and happy. It should mean more than simply cutting the tie to this one person, for that can be done impulsively in fear or anger, with nothing learned. Instead, it should be understood as a major step in coping with your tendency to let your Attachment Hunger rule your life. In all, it should advance you toward a much larger goal—reclaiming full ownership of yourself.

This idea was expressed poetically in the gentle and sensitive book, *How To Survive the Loss of a Love:*

the need you
grew
still remains.

but less and less
you seem the way
to fill that need
I am*

Can I Make It Alone?
    The second kind of question commonly asked is,
"Will I be able to bear being alone? Can I ever feel all
right about being on my own?" I have seen many
people who had fiercely dreaded being without a
primary partner in their lives find that, after the initial withdrawal period, it was not nearly as bad as
they had anticipated. They began to discover the
self-affirming value of it, the "dignity in it" as one
person said. And they could learn the unique pleasures and comforts of being without a prime connection. But you will only come to that point of feeling all
right about being alone if you permit yourself to experience all of it, including some of the initial agony
and depression, and do not rush compulsively and
impulsively into the first attachment that you can
find. Consider that period where you have ended one
relationship and have not begun another as a time to
get to know your own feelings and resources, a precious opportunity to discover the depths of your Attachment Hunger and to learn new, non-addictive
ways to deal with these old and powerful needs. There
have been examples in this book of people who have
gone through the pain of it, the loneliness and desola-
tion, to discover their strengths and their ability to
survive, and who have emerged with a clear sense
that the center of their existence is inside them and

* Melba Colgrove, Harold Bloomfield and Peter McWilliams,
How To Survive the Loss of a Love (N.Y.: Bantam, 1976), p. 93.

not in another person. The value of this endeavor has been stated cogently by Stanton Peele:

> The test of our secure being, of our connectedness, is the capacity to enjoy being alone. The person whose relationships are not compulsive is one who values his or her own company. It is easier to be comfortable with a self that is capable of creating satisfying attachments to life. We then welcome periods of solitude where we can exercise and express that self both in the real world and in imagination. We can take pride in a self-sustenance which, while never total, can withstand many pressures. This self-sustenance also serves as the bulwark for our relationships.*

One aspect of self-sustenance involved addressing yourself to your Attachment Hunger needs as a legitimate and inescapable residue of your infant past and, instead of looking to someone else to take on the job of fulfilling those needs, to learn how to fulfill many of them for yourself. In other words, you must learn to listen to the demands of that inner infant and become, for him or her, the best possible parent you can be—a better parent than you actually had. Being such a good parent involves both nurturance and guidance. You must be good to that child, love him deeply, do nice things for him, tell him things that build his self-esteem and confidence, tell him you will always be there for him and not berate him for being a baby. (After all, he can't help it; besides, he's only one part of you that you can, without hate or anger, prevent from tyrannizing your life.) Though you may in many ways even pamper him, when you stop him from tyrannizing your actions, you are offering parental guidance. And you can also give him such guidance by teaching him that all his needs must not be

---

* Stanton Peele, *Love and Addiction* (N.Y.: Signet, 1975), p. 239.

gratified immediately, that he can cope with the pain of not being gratified, that being alone can be okay, and that he need not and should not seek to attach himself to one particular other person to get his needs met.

When I speak of self-sustenance and self-parenting, I am not advocating an existence of Spartan reclusiveness and celibacy. On the contrary, there can be many people and rich friendships in your life. There can be sexuality and all manner of stimulating new and old activities. The only abstinence required is to abstain from allowing the current vacuum in your life to draw you into any kind of addictive gratification of your Attachment Hunger, be it drugs, drinking, compulsive eating, compulsive promiscuity, or another compulsive "love" relationship. One man said that he felt he was always walking around with his umbilical cord in his hand, looking for someone to plug it into, and he did plug it into the nearest relationship. He learned very little about his own capacity to be alone and self-sustaining. The more you can stop yourself from these desperate attempts to avoid facing your separateness, the more you can experience a mature, self-respecting, almost stately sense of who you are. Nobody could have put it better than Eileen, near the end of her long journey up from addiction.

> I've learned that the only person I can't live without is me. No one else is essential to my survival. "Me" was lost for a long time, wasn't it? . . . I see that I'm going to last forever with myself, so the relationship with me must come first. . . . Now, "alone" has come to mean private, not lonely. Being alone is special.

Will I Ever Have a New Love?
The third type of question deals with new relationships: "Will I ever have another love relationship? And why should it be better than what I have now?"

Very likely you will have another relationship if you want one, though there are no guarantees. You can avoid having one should you so choose. Perhaps that would be a simple preference—or it might be a self-protective reaction to the distress of the last one. You can decide to be reclusive, to be unresponsive to the signals from others, to be hostile, or to make no effort. It would be important to recognize that you are making that choice and not to blame your lack of success in forming new relationships on bad luck, lack of opportunity, etc. But if you are open to a new relationship and make opportunities to meet and be with people, there is a great likelihood that you will have a new love.

Will it be better than the one you have given up? That also will be up to you. It doesn't have to be better. It could even be worse. And there is a good chance it will be at least as bad if you repeat your old unfortunate patterns of selecting partners and old self-defeating ways of interacting with them. The most important thing you should have learned from the ending of the past relationship is an awareness of how you can be influenced by your Attachment Hunger. Specifically, it is essential that you grasp that while your Attachment Hunger comes from childhood when you were *appropriately* dependent, it may now be leading you into relationships where such dependence is *inappropriate* and damaging to both you and the relationship. And you may experience this renewed dependency as if it were true love. But it is not. Dr. M. Scott Peck put it this way:

> . . . dependency may appear to be love because it is a force that causes people to fiercely attach themselves to one another. But in actuality it is not love; it is a form of antilove. It has its genesis in a parental failure to love and it perpetuates the failure. It seeks to receive rather than to give. It nourishes infantilism rather than growth. It works to trap and constrict rather than to

liberate. Ultimately it destroys rather than builds people.*

Perhaps the one point that almost all writers on the subject of love agree on is the destructive impact that childhood dependency feelings can have when they dominate an adult love relationship. Stanton Peele emphasizes the crippling effects of these powerful needs on both parties:

> Because the parties in an addictive relationship are motivated more by their own needs for security than by an appreciation of each other's personal qualities, what they want most from each other is the reassurance of constancy. Thus they are likely to demand unchallenged acceptance of themselves as they are, including their blemishes and peculiarities. . . .
> Such lovers do . . . require each other to change. . . . But the adaptations expected or demanded are entirely toward each other and do not entail an improved ability to deal with other people or the environment. On the contrary, the changes one partner requests of the other to better satisfy his own needs are almost always harmful to the other's general development as a person. . . . In fact, a lessened ability to cope with anything or anyone else is welcomed in the other as a strong guarantee of allegiance to the relationship. . . . It is why an addict actually hopes that his lover will not meet new people and enjoy the world, since this suggests competing ties and interests that would make her less dependent on him.†

So if dependency is destructive to love relationships, what are you to do with the irreducible residue

---

* M. Scott Peck, *The Road Less Traveled* (N.Y.: Touchstone, 1978), p. 105.

† Stanton Peele, *Love and Addiction* (N.Y.: Signet, 1975), p. 85.

of needs from the Attachment Hunger level? Everyone has these needs, though some people have been so hurt by the way they have been handled either in their early childhood or later on that they may have walled off such feelings, perhaps becoming withdrawn or fiercely counterdependent. But the needs are there. You can't exorcise them, surgically remove them, or pretend they do not exist. How can you have these old pulls toward dependency and not become addicted to someone else?

While it is true that you cannot purge your Attachment Hunger level needs, you can increasingly come *to stop yourself from making important life decisions on the basis of them.* You can, for example, stop yourself from marrying someone who may meet many of your Attachment Hunger needs for fusion and security but who is otherwise inappropriate and wrong for you. You can decide to get out of such a relationship more quickly, or not to get into it at all. Doing this consciously and deliberately, while at first requiring much willpower, effort, and determination, by increasing your perspective on the old patterns and the old Attachment Fetish Persons, will, in time, become an automatic aversion to those destructive patterns and persons. And this is half the battle.

The other half of the battle is to develop the capacity to get your particular packet of Attachment Hunger needs reasonably well gratified in ways that are constructive and enhance your growth rather than in ways that are destructive and limiting. I have offered guidelines that indicate the importance of expanding your sources of fulfillment through self-parenting, multiple attachments, and by forming attachments that are more timeless than fragile human relationships (chapter 17). This reduces the weight of the Attachment Hunger that you would put on a single and possibly ephemeral source. But there is no doubt that for the vast majority of people the most satisfying way to meet attachment needs is through an intimate and sustained love relationship. *If you find that your attachment needs have led you into bad relationships, the answer is not in giving up on relationships or in trying to deny your Attachment Hunger. The answer is in changing your old self-defeating patterns of fulfilling your Attachment Hunger to self-enhancing ways of fulfilling it. This requires that you make a conscious effort to form relationships in which your attachment needs are gratified within an interaction that is supportive and strengthening, rather than destructive and weakening.*

And it is here that we find a paradox—*within a love relationship you can best get your Attachment Hunger needs met, and in healthy, dependable, deeply gratifying ways, when your motivation to get those needs met is not primary or controlling.* When you have been able to lessen the grip of that panicky, needy, clinging, possessive, insecure, and devouring baby within you, then you can stand in a relationship that can gratify both your adult needs for companionship, caring, sharing, and support as well as that still remaining portion of your Attachment Hunger. For in any good adult relationship, the baby part of you and of the other person should be able to get held and nurtured on those occasions when such needs are foremost. At one moment one of you can be the needy child and the other the supportive parent, and at the next moment the directional arrows can be reversed. Or each of you at the same time can be both needy and supportive. It enriches and deepens a relationship if it includes this early level of need satisfaction. It becomes malignant and anti-growth only when that mode, the Attachment Hunger dependency of one of you or both of you (with the insecurity, fear of abandonment, and need to control that goes with it), is the overriding dimension of the relationship.

It can be helpful to the growth of each partner to work toward reducing the degree to which Attachment Hunger enters the relationship, even where it is not a particularly dominant part of the relationship. Ken Keyes, in his book *A Conscious Person's Guide to Relationships*, has some interesting things to say on that score. He also uses the term "addiction" but defines it somewhat differently than the way I have used it. He writes:

> When we use the word "addiction," we will be referring to something we tell ourselves we *must have to be happy.* If we don't have it, we will feel emotionally upset. In other words, an *addiction is an emotion-backed demand, model or expectation.* For example, if I get angry when you keep me waiting, I am in touch with an addiction. . . . An addiction automatically creates our unhappiness when the world is not fitting our emotion-backed models of how things should be.*

Keyes goes on to propose that a major task in our growth is to raise an addiction to a preference. "When you work on your addictions and uplevel them to preferences . . . you do not have to change your opinions about life, you do not have to stop trying to change 'what is' and you do not have to necessarily like 'what is.' *It's just that you no longer live with your finger stuck on the emotional panic button."*† Often, upgrading your addictions to preferences can change the relationship and make it unnecessary for you to leave it because it opens the possibility of loving.

The addictive element in our relating (for Keyes, "something we tell ourselves we must have to be happy"; for me, when our Attachment Hunger overrides our judgment and self-interest) can often feel like love, but it is a pseudo love that makes real love impossible. By its very nature it is saying, "I need to be attached to you so that I won't feel insecure, frightened, incomplete, and inadequate, and there-

* Ken Keyes, *A Conscious Person's Guide to Relationships* (St. Mary, Kentucky: Living Love Publications, 1979), p. XIV.
    † *Ibid.,* p. XVI.

fore you must be there and be the way I need you to be in order for me to feel okay." This does damage to the possibilities of loving, because loving involves recognizing and caring about the separateness and the growth of the other person in accordance with his own best unfolding and not your script for him. Loving also involves knowing the other person deeply and fully, but that is impossible if your Attachment Hunger needs distort him into the image you need for fulfillment or if your rage at his not being what you need him to be makes you see him as malevolent or uncaring. *Addiction inevitably, inexorably, drives out love. And non-addictive openness to seeing who the other person is and respecting his separateness permits a loving involvement.* You may then choose, in terms of the total picture of the relationship, whether you wish to have that involvement with that particular person. Keyes contrasts addiction and involvement in this way:

> Addiction means creating emotion-backed demands in my head that dictate what my partner should say or do—it means "ownership." Involvement means that I choose to share a large part of my life with my beloved and build a mutual reality together. Addiction means that I feel insecure without someone—I want him or her to save me. My involvement gives me the opportunity to experience all of the beautiful, loving things that a relationship can bring into my life. It also lets us shoulder together the responsibilities and problems of life and develop a mutual trust. Addiction . . . makes me impose a lot of emotion-backed models of how my partner should be for me to let myself be happy.*

Your chances of finding a new and more enriching love are directly related to whether the insights

Ibid., p. XLIII.

and strengths you gained in the process of becoming unhooked from the last one have reduced your addictive need. If they have not, even the pursuit of a new relationship can be jeopardized, because many people whom you would value would be driven away by your intense Attachment Hunger even before a relationship can really get started. And sustaining a new relationship can be jeopardized by a neediness that constricts and suffocates you and your partner or that allows you to settle for much less than you could have. But if you have learned greater independence and self-regard, if you can value who your partner is and not who you need him to be, then you are *more ready than ever* for a love relationship, and the chances of achieving one are great.

I once wrote of what makes for a good relationship between a parent and his grown-up offspring. The same words can as well apply to a relationship of love partners:

> We are attached by caring, not strings. We stand in a loving relationship at enough distance so that each can see the other clearly in the spankingly crisp space between us and around us, yet close enough to reach out and touch each other with our fingertips or our eyes, close enough to offer a hand in support when it is needed, close enough so that with a single step, we can embrace each other when our feelings call us to it. A loving separateness. It is what a relationship . . . can be.*

Between a Risk and a Certainty

There are risks in ending a bad relationship. You can't know what will happen next. But let us assume you have recognized the preciousness of a continuous and caring partnership and have accepted the neces-

---

* Howard Halpern, *No Strings Attached: A Guide to a Better Relationship with Your Grown-up Child* (N.Y.: Simon & Schuster, 1979), p. 223.

sity of working hard to sustain it. Let us further assume that you have tried to reduce your addictive demands and communicated your adult preferences to your partner. And, finally, let us assume that you have allowed sufficient time for positive change to happen. But you find that despite your patience and your efforts, the relationship remains destructive or unfulfilling. Then, is not the greater risk to your happiness, health, and personal growth in staying in it? If your wish is for a love relationship rooted in the deep pleasure of intimately knowing and being known, of generous mutual caring, of reliable reciprocal backing, then one certain way of *avoiding* having all that is to linger too long in a relationship that does not and probably never will offer you that joy. As the psychiatrist David Viscott put it, "It is better by far to admit that a relationship is so fragmented and the effort needed to put it together is so great and requires so much love and caring not presently or soon likely to be available that the relationship should end."* It can be better to be alone, particularly when being alone is being with someone you like and can count on. It is better to be free to have new experiences and adventures, free to find and create better relationships, free to exercise your right to love and be loved. Despite all this beckoning freedom, it takes much courage to say goodbye to familiar territory, no matter how bleak its landscape, and to move out into lands uncharted. You can fortify your courage with an unflinching focus on what is at stake, because if you see that clearly, the risks involved in breaking your addictive tie and opening up your life will doubtless feel worth the taking.

* David Viscott, *How to Live with Another Person* (N.Y.: Pocket Books, 1976), p. 184.

INDEX

INDEX

INDEX

Physical disturbances, 8, 236
Physical memories (*see* Bodily memories)
Physical needs (*see* Affection; Sexual attraction)
Physical reactions to Attachment Hunger, 32–34
Physical symptoms of addiction, 8, 9
Power, control through, 109–116, 128
Practical Considerations, 14, 21, 22, 165–170, 175
Preference and addiction, 9, 10
Preparing friends for break-up, 210–212
Prison door effect, 2
Psychotherapy, 179, 229–238
  addition to, 234–238
  conditions for, 229, 230
  leaving, 236, 237

Rationalization:
  in marriage-ending, 169, 174
  in psychotherapy, 237, 239
  and self-deception, 4, 5, 101, 122, 154, 206
Re-entry into society, 209, 210
Relationship(s):
  benefit/cost analysis of, 136
  characteristics of, 193
  control in, 109–128, 157
  ending, 135–159
  mature needs in, 156–159, 252
  motives for, 159
  patterns in, 59, 60, 192–195, 231, 251, 252
  rescue operations in, 96, 97
  review of, 192, 193
  Satisfaction Inventory, 137–139, 143
  (*See also* Attachment Hunger; Love; Marriage)
Religion, 131, 132, 173, 226
Rescue operations, 96, 97
Responsiveness of parents, 57, 58
Risk, 255, 256
Rivalry (*see* Competition; Sibling rivalry)

Road Less Traveled, The (Peck), 23n, 250n

Satisfaction Inventory, Relationship, 137–139, 143
Search for Oneness (Silverman et al.), 20n
Self (*see* Identity)
Self, cult of, 149
Self-actualization, 148, 149
Self-centeredness, evaluating, 148–155
Self-deception, 2, 4, 100–108, 179, 186, 230, 239
  (*See also* Rationalization)
Self-esteem, 60–64, 96, 97, 147, 189, 231
Self-indulgence, 185
Self-parenting, 247, 248
Self-sufficiency, 246–248
Selfishness (*see* Self-centeredness)
Sentence Completion exercises, 214, 215
Separation, temporary, 79–82
Servitude, control through, 109, 118–120, 128
Sexual attraction, 85, 86
Sibling rivalry, 75
Silverman, Lloyd, 19, 20n, 129–131
Sleep disturbances, 8
Societal injunctions, 14
Society, re-entry into, 209, 210
Stability, emotional, 65–82
Subliminal perception, 19, 129, 130
Submitting, 113, 114
Survival, 35–37, 39, 47
Symbiotic wishes, 20, 130n, 131–132

Tachistoscope, 19, 20, 129, 130
Tape-recording, 189
Tennov, Dorothy, 22
Therapy (*see* Behavior therapists; Drugs; Psychotherapy)
Thought stopping, 220–223
Time, sense of, 26–31, 240
Timeless, connecting with, 224–228

INDEX